Chemical Dependency and Compulsive Behaviors

Chemical Dependency and Compulsive Behaviors

Richard W. Esterly
Esterly Consulting Associates, Sinking Spring, PA
William T. Neely
Private Practice, West Chester, PA

Routledge
Taylor & Francis Group
LONDON AND NEW YORK

First published in 1997 by
Lawrence Erlbaum Associates, Inc., Publishers
10 Industrial Avenue, Mahwah, New Jersey 07430

Published 2016 by Routledge
2 Park Square, Milton Park, Abingdon, Oxfordshire OX14 4RN
711 Third Avenue, New York, NY 10017

First issued in paperback 2016

Routledge is an imprint of the Taylor and Francis Group, an informa business

Cover design by Gail Silverman

Library of Congress Cataloging-in-Publication Data

Esterly, Richard W.
Chemical dependency and compulsive behaviors / by Richard W. Esterly and William T. Neely.
p. cm.
Includes bibliographical references and index.
ISBN 0-8058-2621-1 (alk. paper)
1.Substance abuse—Etiology. 2. Compulsive behavior—Etiology. 3. Substance abuse—Treatment. 4. Compulsive behavior—Treatment. 5. Addicts—Psychology. I. Neely, William T. II. Title.
[DNLM: 1. Compulsive Behavior—psychology. 2. Compulsive Behavior—therapy. 3. Substance Dependence—psychology. 4. Substance Dependence—therapy. 5. Substance Dependence—etiology. WM 176 E79c 1996]
RC564.E78 1996
616 .86—dc21
DNLM/DLC
for Library of Congress 96-37571
CIP

ISBN 13: 978-1-138-99116-3 (pbk)
ISBN 13: 978-0-8058-2621-0 (hbk)

Contents

Introduction

Our purpose in this book is to further understand the relation between chemical dependency and compulsive behaviors[1] such as gambling, overeating, or sexual acting out. Since the mid 1970s, there has been a marked increase in research on chemical dependency—especially alcoholism—with particular interest in its biochemical and hereditary aspects. Not surprisingly, most of this research has been performed by medically oriented professionals who have had little applied clinical experience.

At the same time, there has been increasing interest in the relation between chemical dependency and compulsive behaviors (or compulsive disorders), most of which is based primarily on anecdotal clinical evidence. Unfortunately, there has been little dialogue between practitioners in these two areas, and whatever dialogue has taken place has generally consisted of discussions of the prevalence and general descriptions of compulsive behaviors and chemical dependency. In addition, there have been fruitless arguments over whether compulsive disorders should be considered "addictions" in the same sense as chemical addictions. We limit the term *addiction* to describe chemical dependency and use the term *compulsive behavior* (or *compulsive disorder* when referring to gambling, overeating, and so forth.

[1]The term *compulsive* in this context should not be confused with the same term as applied to *obsessive compulsive disorder* or *compulsive personality disorder* as defined in the *Diagnostic and Statistical Manual of Mental Disorders* (4th ed.; American Psychiatric Association, Committee on Nomenclature and Statistics, 1994. Diagnostic and Statistical Manual of Mental Disorders, 4th ed. Washington, DC: Author). The only apparent commonality is that, in each instance, the particular behaviors are beyond the individual's voluntary control. The use of a single term to refer to very different disorders can be confusing for health professionals.

This book briefly explores the case for the genetic and biochemical underpinnings of chemical dependency. Based on the authors' study on the empirical relation between chemical dependency and compulsive behaviors and on related research, a new paradigm is presented on how these same or related genetic and biochemical factors may well underlie compulsive behaviors. The paradigm not only explains these relations, but also explores appropriate treatment approaches based on the understanding developed from the model. Specifically, our work addresses the following issues:

1. To what extent is chemical dependency an inherited biological disorder and to what extent is it determined by social and environmental factors?
2. Is chemical dependency a single disease, or are there a number of types of chemical dependency, each having different etiologies that develop in different ways?
3. Is chemical dependency merely another form of compulsive behavior, or does it have unique characteristics that distinguish it from compulsive disorders?
4. What is codependency and what is the relation among chemical dependency, compulsive disorders, and codependency?
5. What are the implications of the theoretical model for developing appropriate treatment programs?

1

Chemical Dependency and Compulsive Behaviors

For a chemically dependent person or a person with compulsive behaviors, life is fraught with pain, misery, broken homes and marriages, and disruptive children. There are also employment and social problems and a myriad of other health, financial, and legal problems. It does not particularly matter if the condition is chemical dependency, a compulsive behavior, or a combination of both. The problems may be extremely severe or relatively mild, and they may or may not be recognized by the person involved. The problems may have existed over a long period of time or they may be of a more recent vintage. Whatever the case, without proper help or treatment, the problems are sure to worsen.

On the basis of our clinical observations and those of our colleagues, we find that in the majority of cases, a strong correlation exists between chemical dependency and compulsive behaviors. In spite of the usually estimated relatively low prevalence of compulsive behaviors in the general population, we estimated that proper assessment of chemically dependent persons would show that at least 50% suffer from one or more compulsive behaviors. The compulsive behaviors that are most correlated with chemical dependency include eating disorders, compulsive sex and relationship problems, gambling, workaholism, stealing, overexercising, and overspending and excessive shopping. Our data, reported in chapter 3, suggest that our original estimate is relatively accurate.

Before we present our theoretical model and supporting data, it would be beneficial to first define and clarify, as much as possible, our understanding of the terms *chemically dependent* (CD) and *compulsive behaviors* and to discuss what is known of the prevalence of each of these disorders.

Chemical Dependency

The American Psychiatric Association's (1994) *Diagnostic and Statistical Manual* (4th ed.; *DSM–IV)* refers to chemical dependency as psychoactive substance dependence. For consistency, we use the term *chemical dependency.* Chemical dependency is defined by tolerance, preoccupation, dependence, loss of control, and craving.

1. *Tolerance* is a state of adaptation in which more of the chemical is needed over time to produce the desired effect.
2. *Preoccupation* occurs as the chemical dependency progresses. More time is spent on activities that involve chemicals. Old friends who do not drink or use other drugs in the same way are left behind.
3. *Dependence* means that a person experiences physical or psychological withdrawal symptoms if the chemical is discontinued. The symptoms are relieved if additional chemicals in the same class (e.g., alcohol followed by either alcohol or other sedative drugs) are taken.
4. *Loss of control* is the inability to stop the chemical intake once it has begun. In the beginning, this is experienced as a "decision" to take more. Loss of control can occur on a daily basis, or the person may go for days or weeks without the chemical. Once the chemical is started, however, the person drinks or uses more than intended.
5. The experienced *craving* during periods of abstinence can lead to additional chemical use or relapse. This craving can be difficult for the nondependent person to understand. The craving is a tension, a yearning that seems to get stronger, if the person does not take his or her chemical of choice.

Using a strict definition of chemical dependency, it is believed that approximately 13% of the adult population is chemically dependent (Rice, Kellman, Miller, & Dunmeyer, 1990). The numbers would be much higher if a broader definition were used to include all individuals who regularly use mood-altering chemicals to cope with life's stresses, even though these chemicals interfere with their ability to function at maximum efficiency. This could include those individuals who insist on cocktails each evening and thus cannot be fully available to help children with homework. Or the weekend drinker or recreational drug user who is unavailable to sit and chat with his or her spouse on a Saturday evening because he or she is too tired after consuming a six-pack of beer or smoking a few joints. Or, it could include the individual who avoids important business commitments early on Monday morning because he or she is slightly hungover and tired from Sunday's festivities.

Although this broad working concept of chemical dependency is probably more relevant for the practicing clinician, for purposes of research it is necessary to limit our definition to more easily measured criteria.

Compulsive Behaviors

Although probably scores of behaviors can be compulsively destructive, only a handful appear with regularity in large numbers of individuals. These behaviors include eating disorders, compulsive sex and relationships, gambling, overspending or excessive shopping, workaholism, overexercising, and stealing.

Compulsive Eating Disorders

Anorexia Nervosa. Anorexics are preoccupied with being thin. They develop a sense of success and control by excessive weight loss, which they feel is an expression of strength and independence (Bruch, 1985). This disorder is generally found in girls and young women between the ages of 12 and 18 and may occur in as many as 1 in every 100 adolescent girls (Hsu, 1980). There is a 5% to 18% mortality rate among victims of anorexia.

Bulimia Nervosa. The essential features of this disorder include recurrent episodes of binge eating, a feeling of lack of control over eating behavior during the eating binges, self-induced vomiting, and use of laxatives and diuretics to prevent weight gain. Binge eating appears to be a way of coping with anxiety and stress, and purging reduces guilt after bingeing (Buchanan & Buchanan, 1992). This pattern results from an overconcern with body shape and weight (Mizes, 1992). This disorder is also most common in girls and young women, affecting approximately 5% of this population (American Psychiatric Association, 1994).

Compulsive Overeating. *Compulsive overeating* can be defined as a harmful, regular pattern of eating more food than one wishes to eat. Compulsive overeaters continue to eat after their appetite has been satisfied, often to the point of physical discomfort. Although there are no direct measures of the frequency of compulsive overeating, a good indirect measure is the occurrence of obesity in the population. Among American adults, some 26%, or 34 million individuals, are obese (Van Itallie, 1985). Even if we assume that only a fraction of these people are truly compulsive overeaters, the prevalence of the problem is still sizable.

Compulsive Sexual Disorders

Compulsive sexual disorders can be defined as a pattern of sexual or relationship behaviors that are regularly used to alter a person's mood. The behavior temporarily alleviates negative affective states such as anxiety, depression, loneliness, and low self-esteem. Compulsive sex and relationship disorders can include sexual behavior such as masturbation, preoccupation with pornography, heterosexual or homosexual relationships, and voyeurism. This disorder can also include a compulsive pattern of "love" relationships, which are actually a compulsion to romantic involvements and usually include sexual activity.

Although the pattern of sexual and relationship behavior can vary dramatically from one person to the next, what is common is that the behavior is destructive and repetitive, the individual is unable to control it without extraordinary effort, and it is used primarily to escape negative emotional experiences. Although there are no reliable estimates of the number of individuals suffering from this disorder, the obvious prevalence of prostitution, pornography, and marital infidelity in our society suggests that the problem is significant.

Compulsive Gambling

The essential features of compulsive gambling are the inability to resist gambling behavior and the fact that it causes financial, family, occupational, or social problems. It is chronic and progressive. The *DSM–IV* (1994, 4th edition) estimates that 2% to 3% of the adult population are compulsive gamblers—although hard data are difficult to come by.

Like other compulsive behaviors, gambling can include a wide range of activities. Most compulsive gamblers engage in the more traditional forms of gambling (e.g., cards, craps, horse racing); however, many may be involved in gambling activities in the financial markets, which is not usually considered gambling by the average person. Regardless of the particular form of gambling, all compulsive gamblers get excited by the possibility of a "big score" that will solve all their problems. This excitement or "high" temporarily alters their mood and results in the distortion of reality and in poor judgment.

As a result, individuals lose control and begin to be preoccupied with gambling to the detriment of the rest of their life. This often brings financial ruin upon the gambler and the family.

Compulsive Spending and Shopping

Clinical observations suggest that the majority of compulsive spenders and shoppers are women. This observation seems to fit socialization experiences in our culture. Krueger (1988) suggested that compulsive spending results from feelings of depression and emptiness and that spending alters one's mood in the direction of euphoria, only to be followed by even more depression. If left unchecked, the cycle can result in bankruptcy and criminal activity.

There are no systematic data available on the prevalence of compulsive spending and shopping in either the general population or in the chemically dependent community, however, the problem is substantial enough to have resulted in the formation of support groups. Compulsive spending and shopping can result in the same kind of financial ruin that is seen with compulsive gambling.

Workaholism

Unlike other compulsive behaviors, workaholism is generally respected in our society. In fact, a workaholic mentality is almost a necessity to succeed in many corporate cultures, as well as in a number of our more highly respected professions (e.g., law, medicine, administration). Unlike many other compulsive individuals, the workaholic is financially rewarded for his or her efforts. The destructive aspects of workaholism are the physical toll on the workaholic and emotional deprivation in interpersonal relationships, especially family life.

Again, there are no data available on the frequency of workaholism, but anecdotal evidence suggests it is a significant problem, especially among men. According to Pietropiento (1986), the workaholic is driven by feelings of inferiority and an insatiable need for approval. Inordinate amounts of time are spent working at the expense of recreation, socializing, and family time. But the workaholic is not primarily driven by financial gains; fear of failure and an avoidance of intimacy are the primary motives. Without help, the workaholic generally suffers serious medical problems at a relatively young age, including high blood pressure, heart disease, and other stress-related illnesses. Divorce and alienation from children are also quite common.

Compulsive Exercising

An individual with a compulsive exercising disorder is preoccupied with a regular exercise routine. He or she rarely skips exercising, even for very good reasons such as physical illness or the occurrence of particular family or work demands that would normally preclude exercising. As in all compulsive disorders, the victim becomes preoccupied with the activity and experiences mounting tension and frustration when unable to engage in the behavior.

Although probably the least destructive of all compulsive disorders, compulsive exercising often results in people insulating themselves from intimate emotional relationships. It also allows people to avoid confronting their own negative affective states, such as depression, low self-esteem, and anxiety.

Perhaps the most difficult task for the clinician is to differentiate healthy exercising from compulsive exercising. The determining factor is the rigidity and lack of flexibility in an individual's approach to exercising. Unfortunately, because of the nature of denial, the patient is often a very poor judge of the inflexibility of the behavior, and it is often necessary for the clinician to consult with family members to get an accurate appraisal. As with other compulsive disorders, estimates of the prevalence of this disorder are uncertain.

Compulsive Stealing

Compulsive stealing or kleptomania is relatively rare in the general population. Although only scant data are available, we know that less than 5% of apprehended shoplifters conform to this pattern (American Psychiatric Association,

1994). The essential feature of compulsive stealing is recurrent strong urges to steal objects from stores, the workplace, or from friends, despite no serious lack of money and no need for the objects.

An Overview of Compulsive Behaviors

Compulsive disorders cover a wide range of behaviors and, within each category, include extraordinary variations. In fact, no two compulsive disorders are alike. Each individual's pattern is unique to some extent. Certain characteristic features, however, can be found in all compulsive disorders.

1. The individual lives in a world of denial and delusion, which can occur in a variety of ways, and minimizes the frequency or extent of the behaviors. Even if the person admits to a particular instance of acting out, he or she generally sees this as an isolated incident "caused" by particular circumstances or outside influences. These rationalizations prevent the person from seeing the underlying patterns. This allows the denial of the fact that the acting out can be attributed to factors within that can be neither understood nor controlled. Even when a compulsive individual is willing to admit that there is a problem, the destructive implications of the behavior are minimized. Thus, a male sex addict who gets three women pregnant in a short period of time can bemoan the irresponsibility of women who fail to take the pill. Or, the overweight compulsive eater who suffers from heart disease and back problems may complain about the incompetence of doctors who have failed to cure her ills. Each of these individuals is in a state of denial that allows him or her to minimize the fact that the behavior(s) is destructive and out of control.
2. The behavior is not under the influence of rational decision-making processes. The person does not "choose" the behavior in the usual sense of the term. There is a driven quality to it, and, if the person resists the behavior, anxiety rises. For individuals who do not suffer from compulsive behaviors, this process is difficult to comprehend and thus leaves them perplexed and frustrated.
3. There is a progression in the intensity of the behavior(s) over time. It may occur more frequently, additional behaviors may be added, or variations of the behavior can develop. For example, the person suffering from a compulsive sex disorder may proceed from using pornography, to regular and frequent visits to massage parlors and prostitutes. The compulsive gambler may progress from an occasional visit to the track, to placing daily bets with the bookmaker. The degree and rate of progression of the behaviors vary tremendously from person to person, and it is very difficult to make many meaningful generalizations.
4. The person is preoccupied with the compulsive behavior even when not directly engaged in it. He or she spends inordinate amounts of time thinking about it and looks forward to the next acting out episode. Compulsive individu-

als plan their lives to ensure that it will be easy to act out their particular compulsion. Some of this planning is so automatic that the individuals are only vaguely aware that they are doing it. Thus, a compulsive overeater may go out of his or her way when driving home just to make it easier to stop by a convenience store for a quick predinner snack. The compulsive sex addict may schedule his whole workday in such a way that he can have a brief interaction with a particular woman about whom he has sexual fantasies.

Summary

In this chapter, chemical dependency and compulsive disorders are briefly defined and clarified. It is clear from this review that chemical dependency and compulsive behaviors share many of the same characteristics (e.g., tolerance, progression, preoccupation). In chapter 2, the background theory and research that served as a foundation for the new paradigm are presented.

Although chemical dependency and compulsive behaviors have been only briefly discussed, they are defined with enough clarity and precision to generate a meaningful empirical study program, which is reported in chapter 3. Discussion of the clinical implications of the relationship between chemical dependency and compulsive behaviors are explored after current research and the new paradigm are examined.

References

American Psychiatric Association. (1994). *Diagnostic and statistical manual of mental disorders* (4th ed.). Washington, DC: Author.

Bruch, H. (1985). Four decades of eating disorders. In D. M. Garner & P. E. Garfinkel (Eds.), *Handbook of psychotherapy for anorexia and bulimia.* New York: Guilford.

Buchanan, L. P., & Buchanan, W. L. (1992). Eating disorders: Bulimia and anorexia. In L. L. L'Abate, J. E. Farrar, & D. A. Serritella (Eds.), *Handbook of differential treatment for addictions* (pp. 165–188). Boston: Allyn & Bacon.

Hsu, L. K. (1980). Outcome of anorexia nervosa: Review of the literature (1954–1978). *Archives of General Psychiatry, 37,* 1041–1046.

Krueger, D. W. (1988). On compulsive shopping and spending: A psychodynamic inquiry. *American Journal of Psychiatry, 42,* 174–584.

Mizes, J. S. (1983, March). Bulimorexia: Clinical description and suggested treatment. Paper presented at the annual meeitng of the Southeast Psychological Association, Atlanta.

Pietropinto, A. (1986). The workaholic spouse: Survey analysis. *Medical Aspects of Human Sexuality, 5,* 89–96.

Rice, D. P., Kelman, S., Miller, L. S., & Dunmeyer, S. (1990). *The economic costs of alcohol and drug abuse: 1985.* San Francisco: Institute for Health and Aging.

Van Italle, T. B. (1985). Health implications of overweight and obesity in the United States. *Annuals of Internal Medicine 103,* 383–388.

2

Background for the New Paradigm

The foundation of the new paradigm rests primarily on the work of C. R. Cloninger and Marvin Zuckerman. Cloninger and his associates studied a large sample of alcoholics and concluded that there are basically two types of alcoholics, each related to a specific set of familial factors (Cloninger, Bohman, & Sigvardsson, 1981) and a personality cluster that has a neurobiochemical basis (Cloninger, 1987). Zuckerman proposed the existence of a personality trait that he called sensation seeking (Zuckerman, 1979a) and conducted a systematic research program concerning the relation between this trait and a variety of other traits and behaviors and the biochemical underpinnings of these traits and behaviors.

Chemical Dependency Types

Dozens of typologies for alcoholics have been proposed over the years (Alterman & Tartar, 1986; Babor & Laurerman, 1986; Skinner, 1982). The work of Cloninger is particularly significant because it incorporates many features of other typologies, for example, familial/nonfamilial (Goodwin, 1979), primary/nonprimary (Winokur, Reich, & Rimmer, 1970), but it goes beyond these other formulations by relating alcoholic types to underlying personality structures based on biochemical factors. In addition, Cloninger's typology has undergone considerable experimental scrutiny and has gained some acceptance in the scientific community.

According to Cloninger, there are basically two types of alcoholics. Type I (which Cloninger referred to as the milieu type) is the most common type and occurs in both men and women. It consists of either mild or severe alcoholism and is characterized by an inability to control drinking once it has started (binge drinking). At earlier stages, Type I alcoholics may go for long periods of time between drinking episodes, but as the alcoholism progresses, this time between drinking diminishes. The development of alcohol-related problems generally does not begin until after age 25 and usually does not involve violence, loss of job, legal problems, or aggressiveness. Feelings of guilt and fear about dependence on alcohol are high in Type I. The fathers of Type I alcoholics are often mild to severe alcohol abusers, and mothers may be alcohol abusers. The parents are rarely involved in criminal activity.

Type II alcoholics are predominantly men (hence, Cloninger referred to them as male limited). Alcohol-related problems occur at a very young age, usually in the teens, and these individuals end up in treatment (often a number of times) before the age of 30. There is a marked proclivity for aggression and antisocial behavior, such as fighting in bars and driving while intoxicated. These individuals rarely abstain from alcohol for any extended period of time and show little guilt or fear about alcohol dependence. The fathers of Type II alcoholics are likely to have a history of criminality and are severe alcoholics themselves (Table 2.1).

Although there is a genetic component to each type of alcoholism, the degree of genetic predisposition varies considerably. Using sophisticated statistical factor analysis, Cloninger concluded that Type I alcoholics are born with the genetic possibility to be alcoholic, but the likelihood and severity of alcoholism depend on environmental factors. Type II alcoholics, on the other hand, are under greater genetic control and have a very high susceptibility to alcoholism. Regardless of the environment, the genetic predisposition almost ensures that, if they drink, alcohol problems will develop.

It is important to bear in mind that Cloninger actually hypothesized the existence of a continuum, with many individuals falling between the pure types. By examining the extremes of each prototypic group, however, the relevant traits that define each type are made more explicit. According to Cloninger, Type I and Type II alcoholics differ on three dimensions of personality. Although the personality clusters were statistically validated, Cloninger hypothesized that each personality is related to an underlying biochemical system. In essence, Cloninger stated that each personality dimension is related to a particular neurotransmitter system in the brain (Table 2.2).

TABLE 2.1
The Relationship Between Types of Alcoholics and Defining Characteristics

Characteristics	*Type I*	*Type II*
Prevalence	Most common	Less common
Sex	Male and female	Predominantly male
Onset	Late	Early
Drinking	Binge	Constant
Criminality	Unlikely	Likely

TABLE 2.2
The Relationship Between Neurotransmitters and Related Personality Characteristics

Neurotransmitter	*Type I*	*Type II*
Dopamine	Low novelty seeking	High novelty seeking
Serotonin	High harm avoidance	Low harm avoidance
Norepinephrine	High reward dependent	Low reward dependent

The first personality trait is novelty seeking, which is related to the neurotransmitter dopamine. According to Cloninger, Type I alcoholics are low on novelty seeking and tend to be rigid, orderly, and attentive to details. Type II alcoholics are high on novelty seeking and are impulsive, exploratory, and easily distracted.

The second trait, harm avoidance, is related to the neurotransmitter serotonin. Type I alcoholics are high on harm avoidance and thus are cautious, apprehensive, pessimistic, and easily fatigued, whereas Type II are confident, uninhibited, carefree, and energetic.

The final trait is reward dependence, related to the neurotransmitter norepinephrine. Type I alchoholics are also high on this trait, which makes them socially sensitive, empathic, eager to help others, and interpersonally available. Type II alcoholics are socially detached, emotionally cold, and independently self-willed. Cloninger's work provides a solid framework for understanding the nature of chemical dependency. The most important conclusions drawn from his research appear valid. Other investigators have found support for Cloninger's typology. Although the involvement of neurotransmitters of the brain in personality types is in line with current scientific theory, the specific neurotransmitters have not been validated. The one consistent finding is that monoamine oxidase (MAO; e.g., Pandey, Fawcett, Gibbons, Clark, & Davis, 1988; Sullivan et al., 1990), which regulates dopamine, serotonin, and norepinephrine, is high in Type I alcoholics and low in Type II alcoholics. A number of recent studies, however, have indicated that the biochemistry underlying the relation may not be quite as simple as first assumed by Cloninger (Roy, Dejong, Lamparski, Adinoff, & George, 1991; Sullivan et al., 1990; Zuckerman, 1991). Our own research causes us to question some of Cloninger's interpretations of his findings, a matter discussed in chapter 3. Cloninger's typology appears to have gained some critical scientific support and seems to meet the criteria for a clinically valid typology as delineated by Penick, Powell, and Othmer (1984):

1. The method should be reliable and stable over time.
2. Developmentally, the course and history should be observable and describable.
3. The prognosis and treatment outcome should vary as a function of the subtype.

Sensation-Seeking Trait

In addition to relying on Cloninger's work, the new paradigm relies heavily on Zuckerman's research program related to the personality trait "sensation seeking." Zuckerman (1979b) defined *sensation seeking* as "the need for varied, novel, and complex sensations and experiences and the willingness to take physical and social risks for the sake of such experience" (p. 10). Zuckerman (1971) developed the following four subtraits related to sensation seeking:

1. Thrill and adventure seeking: This involves risky sports and activities involving speed, movement, and antigravity.
2. Experience seeking: This refers to expanding experience through the mind and senses by pursuing activities such as art, travel, and unconventional lifestyles.
3. Disinhibition: This points to a hedonistic philosophy and extroverted style that values parties and social activities. It also includes a certain cynical attitude, as well as variety seeking in sexual activities.
4. Boredom susceptibility: This entails a strong aversion to monotony, a preference for unpredictability in friends and activities, and a general restlessness when things are not changing.

Zuckerman was one of the first psychological investigators to relate a personality trait to brain chemistry. Specifically, he suggested that sensation seeking was related to levels of certain hormones, as well as to levels of MAO and specific neurotransmitters (for an excellent review of the complex relation between neurology and behavior, see Zuckerman, 1991).

Zuckerman's sensation-seeking trait has generated a good deal of research over the years. It has shown a relatively strong genetic determination (Fulker, Eysenck, & Zuckerman, 1980) and has been related to a number of behaviors, including risky sports (Zuckerman, 1983b); drug use (Kilpatrick, Sutker, & Smith, 1976; Segal, Huba, & Singer, 1980; Zuckerman, 1972, 1983b; Zuckerman, Bone, & Neary, 1972); fast driving (Zuckerman & Neeb, 1980), sexual experience (Zuckerman, Bone, & Neary, 1972) and other risk behaviors (Zuckerman, 1979a, 1979b); responses to sensory deprivation and confinement; volunteering for unusual experiments; gambling; and cognitive, perceptual, and aesthetic preferences (Zuckerman, 1979b). MAO, which is low in sensation seekers, is also low in bipolar manic-depressives (Zuckerman & Neeb, 1979), primary sociopathy (Blackburn, 1969; Cantwell, 1972; Emmons & Webb, 1974; Zuckerman, 1979b) and manic-depressive tendencies in normal populations (Perderson & Mararo, 1970; Zuckerman, 1979b). Mosbach and Lecenthal (1988) demonstrated that the sensation-seeking trait is identifiable at an early age. It is consistently higher among men than women and declines with age (Zuckerman, Eysenck, & Eysenck, 1978; Zuckerman & Neeb, 1980). It appears to be positively correlated with minimal brain dysfunction (DeObaldia, Parsons, & Yohman, 1983; Tarter, McBride, &

Buonpane, 1977; Wood, Reimherr, & Wender, 1976; Wood, Wender, & Reimherr, 1983), aggressiveness, childhood conduct disorder (Wender, Reimherr, & Wood, 1981), and antisocial behaviors (August & Stewart, 1983; Cadoret & Gath, 1978, Cain & Grove, 1980; Loney, 1980).

Although the behaviors of sensation seekers may change over time (e.g., from delinquent behavior to sexual behavior), the underlying sensation-seeking trait is stable (Newcomb & McGee, 1991). In young people, it is associated with dating and self-confidence, smoking, and drinking and other chemical use.

As noted earlier, Cloninger's typology is actually a continuum. The same is true of sensation seeking. In the real world, individuals fall somewhere on a continuum of sensation seeking rather than in one category among discreet, mutually exclusive categories. Naturally, some individuals fall at the extreme ends of the continuum, and although these are probably a distinct minority, they are the very individuals who receive the most attention because they epitomize the trait.

Because of their need for excitement and novelty, sensation seekers are probably more likely than the average person to use alcohol and other mood-altering chemicals, a suggestion that has received some support in the literature (Zuckerman, 1983b). Many sensation seekers, however, may never use chemicals because of cultural and family circumstances. Instead, they will engage in recreational risk-taking behavior such as rock climbing, auto racing, or sky diving. Others may find outlets in less risky activities that they find exhilarating (e.g., sports, exercising, art, or music), or they may engage in occupations that satisfy their needs for stimulation (e.g., trial lawyer, physician, commodity dealer).

Other sensation seekers may use mood-altering chemicals and may even abuse them for a period of time, but they do not become dependent simply because they do not have the genetic predisposition necessary for chemical dependency (Fig. 2.1).

Similarly, certain low sensation seekers may abuse alcohol and other chemicals to alleviate anxiety, but do not develop a dependency if they do not have the appropriate genetic makeup.

With this brief review as a background, it is time to examine the implications of the preceding inquiry on the relation of chemical dependency to compulsive behaviors.

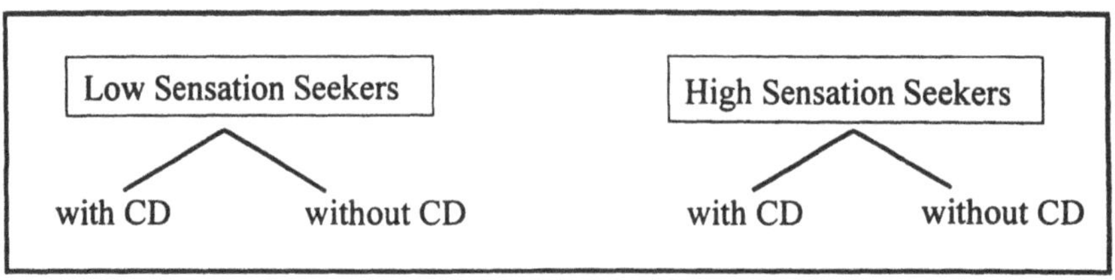

FIG. 2.1. High and low sensation seekers with and without CD. The left side of the figure illustrates the population of low sensation seekers with and without CD. The right side shows high sensaton seekers with and without CD.

References

Alterman, A. I., & Tarter, R. E. (1986). An examination of selected typologies: Hyperactivity, familial, and antisocial alcoholism. *Recent Developments in Alcoholism, 4,* 169–189.

August, G. J., & Stewart, M. A. (1983). Familial subtypes of childhood hyperactivity. *Journal of Nervous and Mental Disorders, 171,* 362–368.

Babor, T. F., & Laurerman, R. J. (1986). Classification and forms of inebriety: Historical antecedents of alcoholic typologies. *Recent Developments in Alcoholism, 4,* 113–144.

Blackburn, R. (1969). Sensation seeking, impulsivity and psychopathic personality. *Journal of Consulting and Clinical Psychology, 3,* 571–574.

Cadoret, R., & Gath, A. (1978). Inheritance of alcoholism in adoptees raised apart from alcoholic biologic relatives. *British Journal of Psychiatry, 132,* 252–258.

Cain, C., & Grove, W. (1980). Development of alcoholism in adoptees raised apart from biologic relatives. *Archives of General Psychiatry, 37,* 651–663.

Cantwell, D. (1972). Psychiatric illness in the families of hyperactive children. *Archives of General Psychiatry, 27,* 414–417.

Cloninger, C. R., Bohman, M., & Sigvardsson, S. (1981). Inheritance of alcohol abuse: Cross-fostering analysis of alcoholic men. *Archives of General Psychiatry, 38,* 861–868.

Cloninger, C. R. (1987). Neurogenetic mechanisms in alcoholism. *Science, 236,* 410–416.

DeObaldia, R., Parsons, O., & Yohman, R. (1983). Minimal brain dysfunction symptoms claimed by primary and secondary alcoholics: Relative to cognitive functioning. *International Journal of Neuroscience, 20,* 173–182.

Emmons, T. D., & Webb, W. W. (1974). Subjective correlates of emotional responsivity and stimulation seeking in psychopaths and acting-out neurotics. *Journal of Consulting Clinical Psychology, 42,* 620–625.

Fulker, D. W., Eysenck, S. B., & Zuckerman, M. (1980). A genetic and environmental analysis of sensation seeking. *Journal of Research and Personality, 14,* 261–281.

Goodwin, D. (1979). Alcoholism and heredity: A review and hypothesis. *Archives of General Psychiatry, 36,* 57–61.

Kilpatrick, D. G., Sutker, P. B., & Smith, A. D. (1976). Deviant drug and alcohol use: The role of anxiety, sensation seeking and other personality variables. In M. Zuckerman & C. D. Spielberger (Eds.), *Emotions and anxiety: New concepts, methods, and applications* (pp. 247–278). Hillsdale, NJ: Lawrence Erlbaum Associates.

Loney, J. (1980). The Iowa theory of substance abuse among hyperactive adolescents. In D. J. Lettieri, M. Sayers, & H. W. Pearson (Eds.), *Theories on drug abuse–research monogram* 30 (pp. 132–136). Washington, DC: The National Institute of Drug Abuse.

Mosbach, P., & Lecenthal, H. (1988). Peer group identification and smoking: Implications for intervention. *Journal of Abnormal Psychology, 97,* 238–245.

Newcomb, M., & McGee, L. (1991). Influence of sensation seeking on general deviance and specific problem behaviors from adolescents to young adulthood. *Journal of Personality and Social Psychology, 61,* 614–618.

Pandey, G. N., Fawcett, J., Gibbons, R., Clark, D. C., & Davis, J. M. (1988). Platelet monoamine oxidase in alcoholism. *Biological Psychiatry, 24,* 15–24.

Penick, E. C., Powell, B. J., & Othmer, E. (1984). Subtyping alcoholics by co-existing psychiatric syndromes: Course, family history, outcome. In D. W. Goodwin, R. T. Van Dusen, & S. A. Mednick (Eds.), *Longitudinal research in alcoholism* (pp. 167–196). Hingham, MA: Kluwer-Nijhoff.

Perderson, L., & Mararo, P. A. (1982). Personality styles and psychopathy. *Journal of Clinical Psychology, 38,* 320–324.

Roy, A., Dejong, J., Lamparski, D., Adinoff, B., & George, T. (1991). Mental disorders among alcoholics. *Archives of General Psychiatry ,48,* 423–427.

Segal, B., Huba, G. J., & Singer, J. L. (1980). *Drugs, daydreaming, and personality: A study of college youth.* Hillsdale, NJ: Lawrence Erlbaum Associates.

Skinner, H. A. (1982). Statistical approaches to the classification of alcohol and drug addiction. *British Journal of Addictions, 77,* 259–273.

Sullivan, J., Baenziger, J., Wagner, D., Rauscher, F., Nurnberger, J., & Holmes, J. (1990). Platelet MAO in subtypes of alcoholics. *Biological Psychiatry, 27,* 911–922.

Tarter R. E., Mc Bride, H., & Buonpane, N. (1977). Differentiation of alcoholics: Childhood history of minimal brain dysfunction, family history, and drinking pattern. *Archives of General Psychiatry, 34,* 761–768.

Wender, P. H., Reimherr, F. W., & Wood, D. R. (1981). Attention deficit disorder (minimal brain dysfunction) in adults. *Archives of General Psychiatry, 38,* 449–456.

Winokur, G., Reich, T., & Rimmer, J. (1970). Alcoholism III: Diagnosis and familial psychiatric illness in 259 alcoholic probands. *Archives of General Psychiatry, 23,* 104–111.

Wood, D. R., Reimherr, F. W., & Wender P. H. (1976). Diagnosis and treatment of minimal brain dysfunction in adults. *Archives of General Psychiatry, 33,* 1453–1460.

Wood, D. R., Wender, P. H., & Reimherr, F. W. (1983). The prevalence of attention deficit disorder, residual type, or minimal brain dysfunction, in a population of male alcoholic patients. *American Journal of Psychiatry, 140,* 95–98.

Zuckerman, M. (1971). Dimensions of sensation seeking. *Journal of Consulting and Clinical Psychology, 36,* 45–52.

Zuckerman, M. (1972). Drug usage as one manifestation of a "sensation seeking" trait. In W. Keup (Ed.), *Drug abuse: Current concepts and research* (pp. 154–163). Springfield, IL: Thomas.

Zuckerman, M. (1979a). Sensation seeking and risk taking. In C. E. Izard (Ed.), *Emotions and personality and psychopathology* (pp. 176–197). New York: Plenum.

Zuckerman, M. (1979b). *Sensation seeking: Beyond the optimal level of arousal.* Hillsdale, NJ: Lawrence Erlbaum Associates.

Zuckerman, M. (1983a). Sensation seeking and sports. *Personality and Individual Differences, 4,* 285–292.

Zuckerman, M. (1983b). Sensation seeking: The initial motive for drug abuse. In E. Gottheil, K. A. Druley, T. Skoloda, & H. M. Waxman (Eds.), *Etiological aspects of alcohol and drug abuse* (pp. 202–220). Springfield, IL: Thomas.

Zuckerman, M. (1991). *Psychobiology of personality.* New York: Cambridge University Press.

Zuckerman, M., Bone, R. N., & Neary, R. (1972). What is the sensation seeker? Personality trait and experience correlates of the sensation seeking scales. *Journal of Consulting and Clinical Psychology, 39,* 308–321.

Zuckerman, M., Eysenck, S., & Eysenck, H. J. (1978). Sensation seeking in England and America: Cross-cultural, age, sex comparisons. *Journal of Consulting and Clinical Psychology, 46,* 139–149.

Zuckerman, M., & Neeb, M. (1979). Sensation seeking and psychopathology. *Psychiatry Research, 1,* 255–264.

Zuckerman, M., & Neeb, M. (1980). Demographic influences in sensation seeking and expressions of sensation in religion, smoking and driving habits. *Personality Differences, 1,* 197–206.

3

The New Paradigm

Introduction

As stated previously, our purpose in this book is to examine the relation between chemical dependency and compulsive behaviors. From the research independently instituted by Cloninger on the types of alcoholics and by Zuckerman on sensation seeking, we propose a new paradigm on the relation of chemical dependency and compulsive behaviors.

The paradigm, presented in brief now and detailed later in the chapter, combines the work of Cloninger and Zuckerman and then builds on this foundation to include a relationship with compulsive behaviors. The paradigm is based on years of clinical observation and some research evidence. The research presented is very preliminary and can certainly be questioned by the astute researcher; however, we hope that the research will be replicated and extended in the future.

The paradigm begins with two assumptions: (a) the types of alcoholics described by Cloninger apply equally to the broader category of CDs, and (b) the novelty-seeking trait described by Cloninger is similar, if not the same, as the sensation-seeking trait described by Zuckerman.

Based on these two assumptions, the paradigm, in brief, asserts that there are two basic types of CDs. Each type has stable, characteristic personality cluster traits and, based on the personality cluster, has a propensity to either high-risk or low-risk compulsive behaviors. Thus, CDs who are low on the sensation-seeking personality cluster (Cloninger's Type I) are less likely to experience compulsive behaviors, and the ones they suffer are low-risk, anxiety-reducing compulsive behaviors, for example, eating disorders, overexercising, workaholism, and excessive shopping and spending. CDs with a high sensation-seeking personality cluster (Cloninger's Type II) are more likely to experience compulsive behaviors, and the ones they suffer are stimulating, high-risk behaviors, for example, sex and relationships, gambling, and stealing.

In this paradigm, the two types of CDs are referred to by the personality characteristic that best summarizes them. Thus, the type with high anxiety is referred to as high-anxiety CDs (HACDs), and the type with high sensation seeking is referred to as sensation seeker CDs (SSCDs).

Although not an integral part of the paradigm, research indicates that imbalances in biochemical neurotransmitters (e.g., dopamine, norepinephrine, and serotonin) are related to personality traits. The same neurotransmitters are also probably related to compulsive behaviors. Most likely, the SSCD experiences a deficit in certain neurotransmitters, and the HACD experiences an excess in the same neurotransmitters (e.g., dopamine, norepinephrine, and serotonin). The use of chemicals or compulsive behaviors stimulates or inhibits the flow of these chemicals and brings the system into balance.

Before continuing with the details of the paradigm, however, it is important to first mention the role of genetic factors in chemical dependency and sensation seeking. First, no intelligent discussion of the types of chemical dependency can occur without addressing this vital area. Second, and even more relevant to our discussion, there appears to be a systematic genetic relation between chemical dependency and the trait of sensation seeking.

There is good evidence that chemical dependency cannot occur without the appropriate genetic predisposition. Certain individuals do not become chemically dependent even if they use and even abuse chemicals with some regularity at certain times in their lives. This is because they do not have the genetic possibility of becoming dependent. For example, many young people abuse alcohol and other mood-altering chemicals in college or in the military. Following graduation from college or discharge from the military, however, they get a job, get married, and reduce their chemical consumption.

According to the best estimates (Rice et al., 1990), approximately 13% of the general population are chemically dependent and, presumably, therefore have some degree of genetic predisposition to chemical dependency. For some, the genetic predisposition is relatively mild, and it may be necessary for them to abuse chemicals for some period of time (5 to 15 years) before they become dependent. Reasons for initial and continuing periods of abuse may vary, but presumably they have to do with a combination of cultural, familial, emotional, and psychological influences.

Other individuals are genetically highly predisposed to chemical dependency and become chemically dependent quickly, following the first chemical use (e.g., in 1 to 2 years). Such individuals can usually vividly recall their first chemical use (usually at a young age) and describe in detail how they felt "normal" for the first time.

There appears to be some natural confounding between the strength of the chemical dependency genetic factors and the sensation-seeking trait. Specifically, individuals who have a high heritability to chemical dependency appear also to

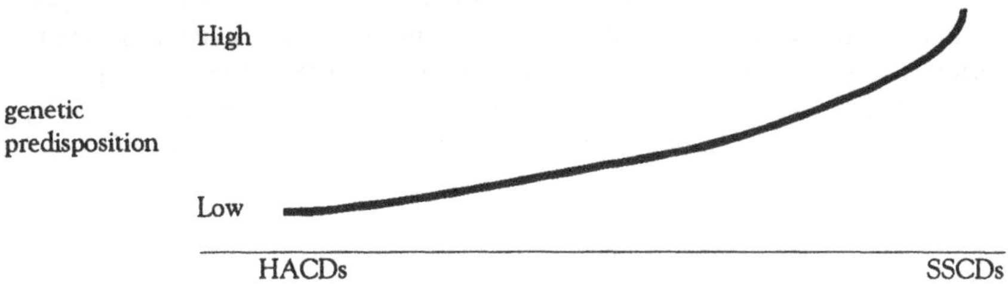

FIG. 3.1. Chemical-dependent types and their genetic predisposition to CD.

have a high heritability to sensation seeking. These high sensation seekers are more likely to experiment with alcohol and other chemicals at an early age and therefore trigger their genetic predisposition for chemical dependency.

On the other hand, HACDs are not as powerfully influenced by a genetic predisposition for chemical dependency and are low in the sensation-seeking trait. They do not experiment as readily with alcohol and other chemicals at an early age, and when they do begin to drink or use other chemicals, they likely go through a period of "social drinking" or recreational drug use before triggering the genetic predisposition for chemical dependency. This relationship can be more readily seen in Fig. 3.1.

The great majority of HACDs are low in the degree of genetic predisposition to chemical dependency, and few, if any, have a powerful genetic component. The reverse is true for SSCDs. The great majority of these individuals have a powerful genetic propensity to become chemical-dependent.[1]

Similarities Between Chemical Dependency and Compulsive Behaviors

The new paradigm begins with two observations. First, there are marked similarities between the nature of chemical dependency[2] and compulsive behaviors. The similarities are striking even to the casual observer.

Each is a disease process that affects its victim physically, emotionally, and spiritually. They are each characterized by preoccupation and craving, with the individual expending enormous amounts of energy, time, and perhaps money in pursuing the chemical or the activity. There is increased tolerance over time, with the individual seeking larger amounts of the chemical or more intense and

[1]The reader will note that the terms *high* and *low* are relative in this discussion. The population being described is the approximately 13% of the population that has the genetic predisposition for chemical dependency.

[2]Although most of the research evidence and theory refers to "alcoholism," we believe that a number of reasons, practical and theoretical, support the use of chemical dependency. Practically speaking, the majority of alcohol-dependent individuals today have a history of multiple drug use. Second, much of the prior research limited itself to alcohol because of funding or personal priorities. Finally, there are biochemical dynamics between alcohol and other chemicals.

powerful substances or experiences to obtain the intended effect. The person continues to use the chemical or to engage in the activity even after he or she knows it is causing problems and in spite of a persistent desire to stop.

In each, withdrawal symptoms occur when the chemical or activity is unavailable. They are both characterized by denial and a world of delusion. Using the chemical or being involved in the activity results in medical problems, accidents, social problems, occupational problems, and family problems. Last, both chemical dependency and compulsive behaviors occur repeatedly within the same families.

The second observation is that both chemical dependency and compulsive behaviors coexist within the same individuals. The majority of CDs suffer from one or more of the compulsive behaviors described in chapter 1. This has long been observed by practitioners in the addiction field, although it has received scant attention from research professionals.

Relationship of Personality and Biochemical Characteristics

On the continuum of individuals with a genetic predisposition for chemical dependency, the HACD (Table 3.1) is distinguished by a lower genetic predisposition for chemical dependency and by related biochemical imbalances, most likely high MAO (von Knooring, Bohman, & Oreland, 1985), dopamine, and norepinephrine and low serotonin. Moderate biochemical imbalances cause the personality characteristics of low sensation seeking and high harm avoidance and reward dependence. More severe biochemical imbalances result in depression and anxiety disorders (e.g., panic disorders, obsessive-compulsive disorders, agoraphobia).

The SSCD has a high genetic predisposition for chemical dependency and has the personality characteristics of high sensation seeking and low harm avoidance and reward dependence. The personality characteristics are also related to a biochemical imbalance—in this case, most likely, low MAO (von Knooring, Bohman, & Oreland, 1985), dopamine, and norepinephrine and high serotonin. A SSCD with a more severe biochemical imbalance may suffer a coexisting sociopathy and more severe depression. This SSCD is also more prone to violence and suicide.

A number of studies have reported the incidence of coexisting psychiatric illnesses with CDs who enter treatment, the most frequent being antisocial personality disorders (extreme SSCD) and generalized anxiety disorders (extreme HACD; Hesselbrock, Meyer, & Keener, 1985; Ross, Glazer, & Germanson, 1988; Rounsaville, Weissman, Kleber, & Wilber, 1981, 1982). There is some evidence that a biochemical imbalance in either extreme causes more serious personality disorders (Siever & Davis, 1991; Zuckerman, 1991). Others have examined the coexisting prevalence of alcoholism and anxiety disorders

TABLE 3.1
The Relationship Between Type of CDs, Estimated Number, Biochemical Imbalance, and Personality Characteristics

The Relationship Between Type and Estimated Number of CDs

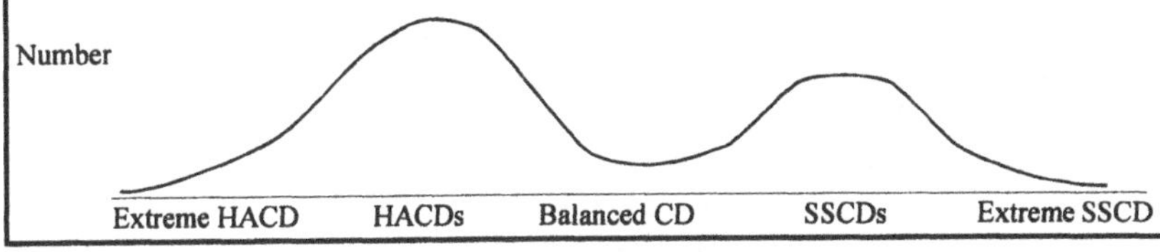

The Relationship Between Type of CDs and Biochemical Imbalance

Extreme HACD	*HACD*	*Balanced CD*	*SSCD*	*Extreme SSCD*
High MAO, dopamine, & norepinephrine, Low serotonin		Normal MAO, dopamine, norepinephrine, & serotonin		Low MAO, dopamine, & norepinephrine, High serotonin

The Relationship Between Type of CDs and Personality Characteristics

Extreme HACD	*HACD*	*Balanced CD*	*SSCD*	*Extreme CD*
Mild depression	Low sensation seeking		High sensation seeking	Depression
Anxiety disorders	High reward dependent		Low reward dependent	Sociopathy
Obsessive/ compulsive	High harm avoidance		Low harm avoidance	

(Weiss & Rosenberg, 1985), panic disorders (Quitkin, Rifkin, & Kaplan, 1972; Smail, Stockwell, & Canter, 1984; Stockwell, Smail, & Hodgson, 1984), obsessive-compulsive disorders (Eisen & Rasmussen, 1989), and the association of antisocial personality disorder with sensation seeking. Unfortunately, these studies did not report the incidence of psychiatric disorders by chemical dependency types (e.g., HACDs and SSCDs).

Additional support for the relation between the catecholaminergic system (dopamine and norepinephrine) and the personality characteristics described with the SSCD and the HACD comes from a related domain—psychopharmacology. Increased levels of norepinephrine have been found to be related to fear, anxiety, and nervousness, and clonidine, a medication that at low doses reduces the activity of norepinephrine has been successful in relieving these symptoms (Uhde & Boulenger, 1984). Clonidine has also been used successfully for opiate withdrawal; is related to anorexia (El-Mallakh, 1992); reduces the withdrawal symptoms of anxiety, tension, irritability, and restlessness associated with smoking cessation (Glassman & Jackson, 1984); and has had preliminary success in treating generalized anxiety disorders (Hoehn-Saric & Merchant, 1981) and posttramatic stress disorder (Kinzie & Leung, 1989).

Women appear to be overrepresented in more extreme HACDs, in which one finds dysthymia (mild depression) and anxiety disorders. Men are more likely to be overrepresented on the extreme right side of the continuum, SSCDs complicated by sociopathy and depression.

Finally, HACDs are more likely to use alcohol and other sedative type drugs because of their tranquilizing effects on anxiety. SSCDs are more likely to use stimulant drugs to satisfy the need for stimulation. Most of the discussion in this book focuses on CDs who do not exhibit the more extreme psychiatric disorders; however, some mention of these more extreme cases is made later in the discussion of treatment and recovery.

Chemical Dependency and Compulsive Behaviors

How does one best account for the fact that chemical dependency and compulsive behaviors are so similar and so often found to occur in the same individuals? Chemical dependency, as noted previously, is related to the sensation-seeking trait. Most likely, chemical dependency, sensation seeking, and compulsive behaviors are all related to the same underlying genetic and biochemical processes. Thus, chemical dependency and compulsive behaviors are both attempts by individuals to bring their neurochemistry into balance. HACDs have an imbalance in certain neurotransmitter systems that results in their feeling continually apprehensive, "on edge," with much anticipatory worrying and hypervigilance, always keeping an eye out for the next catastrophe. For these individuals, alcohol and other sedative drugs and four compulsive behaviors—exercising, shopping and spending, food disorders, and workaholism—help them to reduce their excessive anxiety by lowering tonic catecholaminergic system (dopamine and norepinephrine) activity, thereby lowering their level of behavioral arousal. In other words, they become calmer as a result of the brain chemistry changes induced by these drugs or compulsive behaviors.

In the case of the SSCD,[3] the imbalance in certain neurotransmitters results in underactivity in the catecholaminergic system (dopamine and no-

[3]Although Cloninger (1988) at one point argued that Zuckerman's (1988) sensation seeking dimension is different from his own novelty-seeking dimension, we believe that, for all practical purposes, the two are the same. Moreover, von Knooring (1985) and others used Zuckerman's Sensation Seeking Scale in identifying Type II alcoholics, with positive results. For these reasons, we believe it is justified to refer to Cloninger's Type II chemical dependent as a sensation seeker.

repinephrine). The individual feels vaguely dissatisfied and bored, is easily distracted, highly impulsive, and continually feels the need for behavioral arousal (excitement). These individuals ingest chemicals or engage in risk-taking compulsive behaviors (RTCBs)—specifically, sex and love relationships, gambling, and stealing—to satisfy their subjective needs for excitement. In fact, what they are actually doing is producing increased activity in the catecholaminergic system, thereby raising the arousal level in the brain.

On the other hand, some individuals are chemically dependent but have a relatively balanced biochemical system. These individuals are represented in the middle of the biochemical continuum (see Table 3.1). These CDs do not have the extreme personality characteristics (e.g., harm avoidance, reward-dependence, and sensation seeking). They also are not likely to have coexisting compulsive behaviors. They are not high-anxiety types or high sensation seekers. These individuals are more likely to be the "garden variety" alcoholics uncomplicated by personality disorders and compulsive behaviors.

Research on Chemical Dependency and Compulsive Behaviors

From this theory, it follows that SSCDs are most likely to engage in the three compulsive behaviors that are related to risk-taking: sex and relationships, gambling, and stealing. On the other hand, HACDs are much more likely to engage in the four anxiety-reducing compulsive behaviors (ARCBs): eating disorders, spending and shopping, working, and exercising. Based on this theory, a number of hypotheses were formed and tested:

Hypothesis I: Sensation seekers experience more RTCBs as compared to high-anxiety types.

Hypothesis I–A: Sensation seekers experience more risk-taking than ARCBs.

Hypothesis II: High-anxiety types experience more ARCBs compared to sensation seekers.

Hypothesis II–A: High-anxiety types experience more anxiety-reducing than RTCBs.

A study was conducted to examine this observed relationship between the types of chemical dependency and the types of compulsive behaviors. The study was completed over a 3-month period at a residential chemical dependency treatment facility located in the Philadelphia suburbs. The staff participated in the study as part of their interest in improving the program for patients who were being treated for chemical dependency and who also suffered compulsive behaviors.

First, the Personal History Questionnaire (PHQ; see Appendix A) was developed to divide chemically dependent individuals into the two types (sensation seekers and high anxieties). At the same time, the Compulsive Behavior Inventory (CBI; see Appendix B) was developed to identify seven compulsive behaviors. Specific descriptions from the *DSM-IV* were used in the CBI. For cases in which the *DSM–IV* does not describe a particular compulsive behavior (e.g., sex and relationships, exercising), various professionals assisted in identifying typical behaviors.

To test the reliability of identifying the two types of CDs, skilled clinicians were given a half-day training module on the typologies. The two clinicians most familiar with each patient used their training and clinical judgment to divide the patient population into the two types, SSCDs and HACDs. The two sets of clinicians agreed on 92% of the patients. Thus, when trained, clinicians had little difficulty identifying the two types, and there was substantial interrater reliability.

The next step was to test the validity of the PHQ by comparing the CD types determined by using the PHQ information (obtained from the clinical records by a trained nurse) with the clinical judgments of the trained staff. There was agreement on 88% of the patients. Thus, the PHQ showed very substantial agreement with independent clinical judgment.

To test the validity of the CBI, it was administered to a group of 30 patients. Following the administration of the CBI, the patients were interviewed by trained clinicians. There was 90% agreement between the trained clinicians' judgment of the compulsive behaviors and the CBI. The CBI had a general tendency to underidentify compulsive behaviors, probably due to the denial and stigma associated with the behaviors. The trained clinicians were able to explore questionable areas in depth and to thereby identify valid compulsive behaviors.

Results

Once the two instruments were validated, the next three patient groups (87 patients) who went through the treatment center were asked to complete the two forms. The forms were given to the patients in a group setting following a lecture on compulsive behaviors. The lecture informed the patients about the variety of compulsive behaviors, helped them identify their own, and helped remove the stigma and denial associated with the behaviors.

The results were generally consistent with our expectations. A description of the sensation seekers and high-anxiety types is displayed in Table 3.2.

Our initial results indicate that the two types of CDs can be readily identified with the PHQ. If Cloninger's estimate that 75% of alcoholics in the general population are HACDs and 25% are SSCDs is correct, then it is clear from Table 3.2 that SSCDs are much more likely than HACDs to end up in residential treatment (69% vs. 31%). This may be due to their proclivity for aggression, violence, and criminal behavior. They also are likely to be in treatment at an earlier age (29 vs. 44 years old) than HACDs.

One very interesting difference between our sample and Cloninger's is that in the original work in Sweden, female SSCDs were rare. Cloninger explained this finding by suggesting that women were more likely to suppress their natural proclivity to alcoholism and alcohol-related problems and to experience psychosomatic disorders instead. In the group we studied, however, 41% of the women were SSCDs (12 of 29). This suggests that Cloninger's findings may have been an artifact of cultural factors that do not affect American women.

Overall, 66% of the total group had at least one compulsive behavior. SSCDs are more likely to engage in compulsive behaviors than are HACDs. Seventy-two percent of SSCDs had at least one compulsive behavior compared with only 52% of the HACDs (Table 3.3, a statistically significant result, $p < .03$). SSCDs were more than twice as likely as HACDs to experience at least two compulsive behaviors (41% vs.18%) and were only about half as likely to have no compulsive behaviors (28% vs. 48%). In fact, 11% of SSCDs experienced four or five compulsive behaviors.

In addition, we found in our interviews that SSCDs often experience both consecutive and concurrent compulsive behaviors. For example, one patient was a shoplifter and set fires as an adolescent. As he reached his teen years, he

TABLE 3.2
Selected Demographics of Patient Population by CD Type

	No.	*%*	*% Men*	*% Women*	*% Black*	*% White*	*Age*
N	87	—	58	29	17	70	33
% of total	—	—	67	33	20	80	—
Sensation seekers	60	69	80	20	24	76	29
High-anxiety type	27	31	38	62	10	90	44

TABLE 3.3
Number of Compulsive Behaviors by Percent and Type of CD

	Number of Compulsive Behaviors by Percent					
	0	*1*	*2*	*3*	*4*	*5*
Total (*N*)	34	31	15	12	4	3
Sensation seekers	28	31	17	13	7	4
High-anxiety types	48	33	9	9	—	—

Note. $N = 87$; SSCD: $n = 60$; HACD: $n = 27$.

stopped setting fires, continued to steal, and began a long period of compulsive behaviors related to sex and relationships and gambling.

Although not specifically predicted by the theory, it is not surprising to find that SSCDs are much more likely to engage in a high number of both risk-taking and anxiety-reducing compulsive behaviors. This is analogous to Zuckerman's finding that sensation seekers were more likely than others to abuse drugs of all types, sedative drugs as well as stimulant drugs, although he had predicted they would be more likely to abuse stimulant drugs. Zuckerman suggested that perhaps sensation seekers do not hesitate to find a "high" in almost any drug-taking behavior. If we relate this to compulsive behaviors, although exercising is generally an anxiety-reducing behavior, sensation seekers go for the "runner's high."

Another factor that may contribute to the high number of compulsive behaviors in SSCDs may be intense feelings of guilt and shame associated with morally stigmatized risk-taking behavior. Perhaps the SSCDs use anxiety-reducing behaviors to reduce these intense feelings. This would be analogous to a person "coming down" from stimulant abuse with alcohol and other sedative drugs.

Concerning our specific predictions, Hypothesis I asserted that the SSCDs would be more likely than HACDs to suffer compulsive behaviors related to risk-taking, which we defined as sex and relationships, gambling, and stealing. This is exactly what we found (see Table 3.4).

Fifty-nine percent of sensation seekers experienced RTCBs, whereas only 14% of high-anxiety types did so (statistically significant, $p < .01$). Sex and relationships are by far the most common RTCBs for SSCDs. This may be because sex and relationships are part of our natural instincts, are somewhat socially acceptable, and produce an extreme high. In addition, they fulfill the need for a relationship (see the next chapter on codependency).

Hypothesis I–A predicted that SSCDs would experience more RTCBs than ARCBs. Comparing Table 3.4 and Table 3.5, we see that the SSCDs experienced more RTCBs than ARCBs (59% vs. 43%; statistically significant, $p < .04$).

TABLE 3.4
The Relationship of Risk-Taking Compulsive Behaviors (RTCBs) to Types of CD

	% SSCD	*% HACD*	*% Total*
Sex/relationships	48	4	34
Gambling	20	—	13
Stealing	20	9	16
At least one RTCB[a]	59	14	45
No RTCB	41	86	55

Note. $N = 87$; SSCD: $n = 60$; HACD: $n = 27$.

[a]This row does not equal the above rows because it only counts individuals once (e.g., 59% of the SSCDs have at least one RTCB). The rows above include individuals with multiple RTCBs.

TABLE 3.5
Relationship of Anxiety-Reducing Compulsive Behaviors (ARCBs) to Types of CDs

	% SSCD	*% HACD*	*% Total*
Eating	11	19	13
Shopping/spending	28	19	25
Working	32	31	31
Exercising	9	4	7
At least one ARCB[a]	43	52	46
No ARCB	57	48	54

Note. $N = 87$; SSCD: $n = 60$; HACD $n = 27$.
[a]This row indicates patients with at least one ARCB (e.g., 52% of the HACDs have at least one ARCB). The rows above include individuals with multiple ARCBs.

Although the difference was as predicted, it was somewhat surprising that the difference was not even greater. Again, this finding may result from the unexpectedly high level of ARCBs among the SSCDs. If the same pattern holds in future research, it will be interesting to look more closely at SSCDs and compulsive behaviors that we have identified as anxiety-reducing. Do SSCDs turn everything into a risk or a "high" to satisfy their craving for excitement, or do they become more susceptible themselves to struggles with shame and guilt over time?

Hypothesis II postulates that HACDs are more likely to experience ARCBs (eating, shopping and spending, working, and exercising) than SSCDs. Although our results were in the right direction, Table 3.4 indicates that SSCDs are almost as likely to have ARCBs as HACDs (43% vs. 52%; statistically not significant; $p > .22$). The rationale for this observation was discussed earlier.

Hypothesis II–A predicted that HACDs experience more ARCBs than RTCBs. In fact, HACDs were almost four times more likely to have anxiety-reducing as risk-taking behaviors (52% vs. 14%; statistically significant; $p < .01$). This was, by far, our most strongly supported prediction, and it demonstrates quite clearly that HACD types appear to be extremely averse to risk-taking.

In summary, the four hypotheses were supported. The only hypothesis that was not strongly supported was the contention that SSCDs would exhibit significantly more RTCBs than ARCBs. Although the finding was in the right direction, the difference was not very large. Possible explanations for this observation were offered.

Later in this book, we illustrate the relation between chemical dependency and compulsive behaviors in greater detail with descriptions, case histories, and treatment implications. But first, the important relation among chemical dependency, compulsive behaviors, and codependency must be explored.

References

Cloninger, C. R. (1988). Letters to the editor. *Archives of General Psychiatry, 45,* 503–504.

Eisen, J. L., & Rasmussen, S. A. (1989). Coexisting obsessive compulsive disorders and alcoholism. *Journal of Clinical Psychiatry, 50,* 96–98.

El-Mallakh, R. S. (1992). The use of clonidine in psychiatry. *Resident and Staff Physician, 38,* 29–34.

Glassman, A. H., & Jackson, W. K. (1984). Cigarette craving, smoking withdrawal and clonidine. *Science, 226,* 864–866.

Hesselbrock, M. N., Meyer, R. E., & Keener, J. J. (1985). Psychopathology in hospitalized alcoholics. *Archives of General Psychiatry, 42,* 1050–1055.

Hoehn-Saric, R., & Merchant, A. F. (1981). Effect of clonidine on anxiety disorders. *Archives of General Psychiatry, 38,* 1278–1282.

Kinzie, J. D., & Leung, P. (1989). Clonidine in Cambodian patients with posttraumatic stress disorder. *Journal of Nervous and Mental Disease, 177,* 546–550.

Quitkin, F. M., Rifkin, A., & Kaplan, J. (1972). Phobic anxiety syndrome complicated by drug dependence and addiction. *Archives of General Psychiatry, 27,* 159–162.

Rice, D. P., Kelman, S., Miller, L. S., & Dunmeyer, S. (1990). *The economic costs of alcohol and drug abuse: 1985.* San Francisco: Institute for Health and Aging.

Ross, G. E., Glaser, F. B., & Germanson, T. (1988). The prevalence of psychiatric disorders in patients with alcohol and other drug problems. *Archives of General Psychiatry, 45,* 1023–1031.

Rounsaville, B. J., Cacciola, J., Weissman, M. M., & Kleber, H. D. (1981). Diagnostic concordance in a follow-up study of opiate addicts. *Journal of Psychiatry Research, 16,* 191–201.

Rounsaville, B. J., Weissman, M. M., Kleber, H. D., & Wilber, C. (1982). Heterogeneity of psychiatric diagnosis in treated opiate addicts. *Archives of General Psychiatry, 39,* 161–166.

Siever, L., & Davis, K. (1991). A psychobiological perspective on the personality disorders. *American Journal of Psychiatry, 148,* 1647–1658.

Smail, P., Stockwell, T., & Canter, S. (1984). Alcohol dependence and phobic anxiety states: I. A prevalence study. *British Journal of Psychiatry, 144,* 53–57.

Stockwell, T., Smail, P., & Hodgson, R. (1984). Alcohol dependency and phobic anxiety states: II. A retrospective study. *British Journal of Psychiatry, 144,* 58–63.

Uhde, T. W., & Boulenger, J. P. (1985). Fear and anxiety: Relationship to noradrenergic function. *Psychopathology, 17,* 8–23.

von Knooring, A. L., Bohman, M., & Oreland, L. (1985). Platelet MAO activity as a biological marker in subgroups of alcoholism. *Acta Psychiatrica Scandinavica, 72,* 51–58.

Weiss, K. J., & Rosenberg, D. J. (1985). Prevalence of anxiety disorders among alcoholics. *Journal of Clinical Psychiatry 46,* 3–5.

Zuckerman, M. (1988). Letters to the editor. *Archives of General Psychiatry, 45,* 502–503.

Zuckerman, M. (1991). *Psychobiology of personality.* New York: Cambridge University Press.

4

Codependency

The term *codependency* developed within the field of alcoholism rather than within the mental health field. Although it is not clear exactly when and by whom the term was coined, it most likely developed from the term *co-alcoholic,* referring to a person having a close relationship with an alcoholic. These individuals tend to have certain characteristics, such as low self-esteem, a strong desire to be needed, great tolerance for suffering, and a strong need to control and change others.

Initially, it was assumed that these characteristics developed from living with an alcoholic person. Eventually, it became apparent that, although life with an active alcoholic certainly caused stress and contributed to a variety of psychological problems, many co-alcoholics or codependents had many of the same problems before they ever became involved with the alcoholic. Moreover, they continued to have the same problems after the alcoholic was sober and in recovery or had left the relationship.

Two other interesting phenomena also became apparent. First, in addition to emotional and interpersonal problems, many codependents suffered from compulsive behaviors of their own, such as overeating, overspending, and gambling.

Second, some alcoholics in recovery began to show many of the same characteristics as their codependent partners, including compulsive behaviors.

The pervasiveness of codependence in recovering alcoholics and their families led a number of leading theorists in the chemical dependency field (e.g., Cermak, 1986; Schaef, 1986; Wegscheider-Cruse & Cruse, 1990) to conclude that codependency is the primary disease process in chemically dependent families and generally precedes chemical dependency. Moreover, because of the pervasiveness of compulsive behaviors in codependents, it was concluded that compulsive behaviors and chemical dependency were merely symptoms, along with other symptoms of the disease process of codependency.

These points were made most explicitly by Wegscheider-Cruse and Cruse (1990), who suggested that codependency is a brain disorder that leads to the establishment of compulsive and addictive behavior processes. In addition, they argued that low self-esteem, dependent relationships, and caretaking—those very characteristics that were originally the defining traits that led to the establishment of the term *codependency*—are merely "complications" of this disease process.

Codependency Reformulated

Codependency is a valid descriptive term that is extremely useful in describing certain behaviorally and emotionally disordered people. There is insufficient justification, however, for describing it as a disease process caused by deficiencies in brain chemistry. Moreover, the presence of compulsive behaviors should not be included as a defining characteristic of codependency, although these conditions often go hand in hand. Instead, the term *codependency* is best defined in terms of low self-esteem and certain types of disordered interpersonal relationships that result from being raised in a dysfunctional family.

Because the term *codependency* developed within the chemical dependency field and perhaps because those who were instrumental in defining the term were unfamiliar with the broader mental health field,[1] unwarranted conclusions seem to have been drawn on the basis of a limited population. Because they were familiar only with a narrow type of dysfunctional family, namely, alcoholic families, they assumed that there was a necessary relation between alcoholism and codependency.

More recently, it has been recognized that many dysfunctional families are not alcoholic (or even chemically dependent) and that in those families codependency is just as prominent. Similarly, because compulsive behaviors are so common in chemically dependent families, many people erroneously concluded that compulsive behaviors are another defining characteristic of codependency. Again, in dysfunctional families that are not chemically dependent, we find codependents who do not experience compulsive behaviors.

How then would we define codependency? Quite simply, codependency is a disorder in the bonding process between parent and child. It results from being raised in a dysfunctional family environment and exists in a person to the extent that his or her level of self-satisfaction and serenity is determined, almost exclusively, by the behavior, attitudes, and feelings of significant others.

---

[1]For too many years there has been minimal communication between specialists in chemical dependency and those in mental health. This was understandable when mainstream mental health therapy was primarily insight oriented. Chemical dependency specialists realized that insight into chemical dependency did little to alter that disease. Psychological theory and practice have changed radically, however, and a number of theorists (e.g., Watzlawick, 1978) have recognized that it is often necessary to change destructive behavior before one can begin to undergo meaningful psychological growth.

Attachment Theory

In the 1950s, John Bowlby, a British psychologist, was commissioned to study and report on the effects of the separation of children, either temporarily or permanently, from their mother figure. Bowlby (1973) concluded "that many forms of psychoneurosis and character disorders are to be attributed either to deprivation of maternal care or to discontinuities in a child's relationships with his mother figure" (p. vi).

To explain their findings, Bowlby and his colleagues went on to develop attachment theory (Bowlby, 1969, 1973, 1980). Attachment theory is a theory of personality development that states that many animal species, especially humans, have an instinctive need to develop affectional bonds with specific members of their species. Initially, this bond is with the mother figure, and later it is with others. In humans, the formation, maintenance, and disruption of the affectional bonds evoke some of the most intense emotional experiences people can have. In common parlance, these experiences are described by such terms as *falling in love, being in love,* and *mourning a loss.*

Adult personality, at least in part, is seen as a product of a person's key attachment figures during the childhood years; however, this process, which results in adults' often behaving in terms of their early bonding experiences, is not simply a mindless, reflexive affair that "just happens." Instead, it is a result of the beliefs and attitudes—a working model—that children develop regarding the nature of their world and how they fit into this world. The purpose of the working model is to make sense of the experience that the child has.

The most central determining factor in the development of the working model is the availability and responsiveness of significant attachment figures. First, they must be regularly available. Second, they must be reasonably responsive to the child's needs and they must be responsive in a particular way. They must feel some joy and satisfaction in being able to provide for the child's needs. Otherwise, their "caring" is nothing more than the fulfillment of another tedious obligation, and the child senses that he or she is a burden.

If these conditions are met for the most part (all parents have some days when their children feel burdensome), then children will develop an almost unconscious assurance that there will always be some trustworthy figures available in their life in times of need. They will make sense of this belief by attributing it to the fact that they are persons who are worthy of being cared about and helped. In short, they are loveable. Such children naturally grow up to be adults with an extremely positive self-concept who approach life with confidence.

On the other hand, those who have not had the experience of consistently available parent figures who responded to their needs freely and with affection develop a view of the world as a comfortless and potentially dangerous place. They have difficulty finding joy in life because joy comes to those who first feel safe and secure. Naturally, such children can only conclude that they are essentially unwanted and unlovable. What other possible explanation could occur to the young child whose parents either are not there or do not seem to care when they are there.

Attachment Disorder—A Perspective on Codependence

According to Bowlby, disturbances in early attachment commonly result in predictable emotional distress that includes anxious attachment, compulsive caregiving (which is a variation of anxious attachment), and emotional detachment (which is usually partial but, in rare instances, can be complete).

The most common emotional disturbance that results from attachment disturbances is *anxious attachment*. Individuals suffering from anxious attachment grew up in families in which there were attachment figures, but these figures were unavailable or unresponsive on a regular basis. Therefore, they could not be depended on. As a result, children from these families grow up to be adults who are chronically anxious and unsure of themselves and are likely to exhibit exaggerated forms of attachment behavior; that is, they are overly dependent on others and continually look to others to assure themselves that they are okay and will not be abandoned.

Unfortunately, such individuals are subject to ridicule and disparagement for being so "weak" and "dependent." Even in the mental health field we categorize people as having "dependent personality disorders," thus adding to the shame that these individuals already experience. If we instead remind ourselves that so-called dependent behavior is nothing more than an exaggerated expression of normal attachment behavior in a person whose childhood attachment behavior was not adequately responded to, then we remove much of the unnecessary stigma and, at the same time, are more accurate in our description.

Compulsive caregiving is, according to Bowlby, a variation of anxious attachment. Compulsive caregivers concern themselves almost exclusively with the welfare of others while remaining oblivious to their own needs. They usually experience high levels of free-floating anxiety, which they believe results from their concerns for their loved ones. They typically have little insight into themselves and are unaware of their own low self-esteem. They seem to try to feel okay about themselves by selecting partners in life who are obviously handicapped or in some sort of trouble and then by taking care of them. Not only does this give them a reason to feel worthwhile, but it probably also represents an unconscious attempt to nurture themselves by projecting their own needs on others. Unfortunately, these patterns of behavior assure a life of frustration marked by continual disappointment and an ever-increasing hostility (sometimes unconscious) toward those whom they caretake.

Compulsive caregivers also come from families characterized by certain types of inconsistencies in the responsiveness of attachment figures. The pattern is found particularly in families in which there was a curious denial of many of the child's legitimate emotional needs because of a preoccupation with the unhealthy emotional needs of one or both of the parents. Probably the most common pattern occurs in a family with an anxiously attached mother and a father who is emotionally distant and who abandons his wife either by spending most of his time away from home or by being emotionally unavailable when he is at home.

In such a family, typically there is a reversal of the usual child–parent relationship, with the child caring for the mother and sometimes for the siblings. In order to be the caretaker, the child naturally has to suppress many of her or his own legitimate emotional needs in favor of the needs of the parent. In return, the child gets some opportunity to be close to mom and usually receives much praise and appreciation from dad, who no longer has to deal with his wife's demands.

The third type of emotional disorder resulting from disturbance in early attachments is what Bowlby called *emotional detachment.* Unfortunately, the word *detachment* can be confusing because its meaning in the addiction field differs from that given by Bowlby. Bowlby referred to a defensive process whereby children protect themselves from experiencing the anxiety that results when they experience overwhelming losses in relation to an attachment figure. These can include the death of a parent, extreme neglect, or an extremely abusive attitude in response to a child's need for love and affection. The child then "detaches" or suppresses his or her needs for affection and becomes almost completely unaware of them.

In extreme instances, children may develop a "schizoid" personality disorder in which the emotional need for others is entirely absent throughout their lifetime. In most instances, however, the suppression is only partially successful—the affectional need system is only partially deactivated—and just below the surface there remains an overpowering need to be loved and cared for. In these cases, the children must learn to avoid situations that might lead to their feeling a need for affection from others. Therefore, they adopt a strategy of compulsive self-reliance whereby they assiduously avoid anything even remotely resembling a vulnerable position in a relationship. Such individuals appear emotionally invulnerable, and, for all practical purposes, they are. If, for any reason, they find themselves beginning to experience a desire for love or support, they become overwhelmed with shame and immediately distract themselves, usually by getting angry.

Codependency as an Attachment Disorder

Bowlby's description of anxious attachment and compulsive caregiving is almost identical to the literature describing the interpersonal characteristics of the codependent: rigid, anxious, overly dependent, people-pleasing, caretaking, and so forth. What is not as readily apparent is the relation between the concept of codependency and Bowlby's "detached" type.

The connection is less apparent because not enough attention has been paid to the fact that there are two distinctive and, in some ways, very different interpersonal expressions of codependence. Remember, persons are codependent to the extent that their level of self-satisfaction and serenity is determined primarily by the behavior, attitude, and feelings of significant others. The first, and more typical interpersonal style that we think of, is the person who usually seeks professional help, namely, the "people-pleaser" who displays ingratiating, overly dependent, solicitous behavior characteristic of the anxiously attached and the compulsive caregiver.

There is a second codependent style, however, which is less commonly seen by mental health professionals and that corresponds to Bowlby's detached type. We refer to this individual as the "bullying type." Bullies are just as dependent as the people-pleaser on the behavior, attitudes, or feelings of significant others to feel okay about themselves; however, they try to control others through anger and intimidation. These individuals—in the majority of cases, men—are out of touch with their own affectional needs and substitute controlling others for their own unconscious yearnings to be loved and affirmed. They may or may not be aware of the extent to which they intimidate others, but they are aware that they usually feel "one down" and vulnerable much of the time. By controlling others through anger and intimidation, they feel less vulnerable because they keep people at a safe distance and yet assure that they will not be abandoned. Unfortunately, their "victories" assure that their underlying loneliness and emotional hunger are never satisfied.

Codependency, Chemical Dependency, and Compulsive Behaviors

Understanding codependency as an expression of an early childhood attachment disorder readily explains why codependency is typically found in chemically dependent families. Family stresses resulting from chemical abuse and compulsive disorders are readily observed. Healthy parenting can hardly be expected to occur in families that are struggling to survive. This results in children whose attachment needs are never adequately satisfied and who develop lifelong codependent coping styles that, when combined with genetic predisposition, almost guarantee another generation of chemical dependency and compulsive disorders. In subsequent chapters we look more closely at the role of codependence in the development and maintenance of chemical dependency and compulsive disorders as well as the necessity of dealing with codependency in any meaningful recovery program.

Conclusions

The phenomenon of codependency, which has proven to be so useful in the recovery field, has received little recognition in the mental health field. We believe this has resulted from two factors. First, the term has never been well defined and has meant various things to different writers. As a result, too much has been included under the rubric of "codependency," to the point where the term has lost its precision.

We do not believe that compulsive behaviors should be listed as one of the defining traits of codependency, although codependent individuals often suffer from compulsive disorders as well as from chemical dependency. Moreover, we believe that attempts to define codependency as a biological disease with various and sundry symptoms are scientifically untenable. We hope that our attempt to define codependency in a more limited way, which is, incidentally, closer to its original usage, will help to clarify its meaning and result in greater acceptance by a broader audience.

The second reason that the term codependency has not been more generally accepted is that, until now, no attempt has been made to discuss the term in the context of a larger psychological paradigm. We hope that this discussion of codependence in terms of Bowlby's attachment theory will remedy that shortcoming and result in greater scientific acceptance as well as a systematic program of research.

References

Bowlby, J. (1969). *Attachment.* New York: Basic Books.

Bowlby, J. (1973). *Separation: Anxiety and anger.* New York: Basic Books.

Bowlby, J. (1980). *Loss: Sadness and depression.* New York: Basic Books.

Cermak, T. L. (1986). *Diagnosing and treating co-dependence.* Minneapolis, MN: Johnson Institute Books.

Schaef, A. W. (1986). *Co-dependence: Misunderstood and mistreated.* San Francisco: Harper & Row.

Watzlawick, P. (1978). *The language of change: Elements of therapeutic communication.* New York: Norton.

Wegscheider-Cruse, S., & Cruse, J. (1990). *Understanding co-dependence.* Dearfield Beach, FL: Health Communications.

5

Overview of Treatment and Recovery

Each chemically dependent person presents unique challenges to the professional. Each requires an individually tailored treatment plan based on a unique biochemistry, personality, family history, and current situation. The therapist must sort out those factors that are most relevant to an individual's recovery from those that are less important. The model presented in this chapter serves as a framework for determining factors that are most important and that need to be addressed in developing a meaningful recovery program.

The model considers recent findings in heredity and brain chemistry, along with relevant personality variables. It presents a meaningful typology that allows the clinician to begin to understand the factors most relevant to any individual's chemical dependency. It offers practical guidelines for making appropriate diagnostic decisions. On the basis of those decisions, the framework allows the clinician to determine the direction that the treatment plan should take and addresses particular complications that may arise in a person's recovery. It places particular emphasis on evaluating and dealing with compulsive behaviors, which may be the greatest threat to an individual's recovery as well as his or her general well-being.

Before beginning the discussion of treatment of the HACD and SSCD, a number of important therapeutic principles, observations, and practices that apply to all chemical dependents are briefly described. These apply to both HACDs and SSCDs and form the foundation of treatment for any CD. In the following chapters, these principles, observations, and practices are more precisely described as they specifically relate to the HACD and SSCD.

Assessing the Chemical Dependent

The first step for the clinician is to determine where on the sensation seeking–high-anxiety continuum a particular person falls. Proper diagnosis is crucial for developing a meaningful treatment plan. In addition, it is necessary to evaluate the presence and extent of compulsive behaviors in the recovering person's life.

The PHQ and the CBI allow the clinician to evaluate the degree of chemical dependency, the type of chemical dependency, as well as the number and type of compulsive behaviors, in a structured and standardized manner. The PHQ, the CBI, and scoring sheets are included in the appendixes.

With patients who have progressed to the point of recognizing their chemical dependency, both inventories can be administered at the same time and completed in less than 20 minutes, either during a therapy session or at home. Having patients fill out the inventories in the office is preferred because it allows the therapist to judge the patient's emotional reaction, answer any questions, and ask follow-up questions as appropriate. This is especially important if patients are still new in treatment, in denial about their chemical dependency, or not entirely comfortable with the therapist. In this case, the PHQ should be administered first.

The PHQ is very easy to administer. Section A evaluates chemical dependency and determines the degree of severity (based on the *Diagnostic and Statistical Manual of Mental Disorders* [3th ed., rev.; *DSM–III–R*]). Section B and Section C determines the type of CD. After patients have completed the PHQ, they should have an opportunity to discuss it during the session. Our experience is that most patients are not threatened by the inventory and answer it truthfully. The CBI is a very helpful screening instrument for quickly identifying both past and current compulsive behaviors.

Generally, a patient can complete the CBI in 8 to 12 minutes. Again, as in the PHQ, the CBI may be either administered during a counseling session or simply given to the patient to complete between sessions.

Early Recovery

It is important to point out the difference between early and long-term recovery in treating chemical dependency because such an understanding is crucial for determining appropriate clinical interventions.

Basically, these periods differ in their goals. The goal of early recovery is to help individuals function without using chemicals. This means that people can adequately fulfill their obligations to their families and their jobs and be responsible for their own welfare without resorting to the use of chemicals. This does not mean optimal functioning, merely adequate functioning. Because this is always a difficult transition period for recovering persons and the family, it is crucial that they receive as much support as possible from others, especially from the therapist and from other recovering people in Alcoholics Anonymous (AA) and/or other 12-step programs.

Ideally, the therapist would like the person to consciously accept the chemical dependency and ask for a list of AA meetings or other appropriate 12-step meetings. Rarely does this occur.

Initially, it is usually counterproductive to insist that a resistant patient accept the label *alcoholic* or *chemical-dependent.* What is crucial is commitment to not drinking or using other drugs for whatever reason that makes sense to the patient at that time.

One of the most important decisions that a clinician must make concerns the appropriate level of care (e.g., inpatient, residential, outpatient, or intensive outpatient). Generally, the therapist has a good idea of the level of care needed for an individual. In making this decision, the criteria developed by the American Society of Addiction Medicine are growing in recognition and acceptance. Patients generally have strong opinions about the level of care they want. Generally, they prefer less intense interventions than are indicated. Occasionally, a therapist must insist on the recommended level of care or otherwise refuse to work with the patient. More frequently, the therapist can be more flexible and accept the patient's desire, but can make a contract whereby the patient agrees to a more intense level of care if there is a relapse.

Unfortunately, in today's insurance environment, a third-party (e.g., insurance or health maintenance organization) utilization review person may be involved in directing the treatment plan and level of care. This makes a comprehensive history, assessment, and exploration of compulsive behaviors and other potential, complicating issues such as psychiatric conditions all the more important. Sometimes, complicating factors help to obtain the appropriate level of care and approval for payment.

If the patient is appropriate for, or insists on, outpatient counseling, then attending an early recovery treatment group is a very important aspect of treatment. If the individual already recognizes that he or she is chemically dependent, then the group serves as a source of identification and support. If the person is still in denial, then a connection with other group members may facilitate identification and make the illness easier to accept.

Occasionally, a therapist may have patients attend a group in which everyone is more progressed in the disease in the hope that they will see what might happen to them if they do not change. However, this strategy often backfires, and the plight of fellow members convinces the patients that they are not "that bad" and thereby increases their denial. Thus, it should be used only when more orthodox means of addressing patients' denials have failed.

Treatment in early recovery should focus on exploring the seriousness of the chemical dependency, identifying oneself as a chemical-dependent, and attending 12-step fellowship programs. The therapy should be supportive in nature. Whether individual, group, or family therapy, the goal is to teach the recovering person and family to deal adequately with life's demands (e.g., solving practical problems, financial counseling, basic communication skills, coping with frustration) without using chemicals. Unless it is absolutely necessary for sobriety, counseling should avoid issues that are likely to put additional stress on the individual. Thus, examining issues such as early family dynamics, long-term marital conflicts, compulsive disorders, and issues relating to sexual intimacy and psychological growth should usually be deferred.

Sometimes, however, very difficult issues must be dealt with in early recovery, or they threaten sobriety. For instance, a married client having sexual affairs could risk losing the marriage. Unfortunately, there are no cookbook formulas for making such decisions. Common sense and clinical acumen are the primary guides. Often, there are no easy answers; however, the clinician who does not forget that the goal of early recovery is to help the patient and the family to function adequately (not optimally) without the use of chemicals is less likely to make errors.

A serious issue that arises when diagnosing CDs in early recovery is that much of their behavior and psychological makeup during their active chemical addiction and in early recovery may be a by-product of their chemical dependency. Thus, high levels of depression and anxiety may be prominent during active addiction and become even more prominent in early recovery. These symptoms may go away after a brief period of sobriety and may not return. Similarly, people who act in ways that would qualify them as sociopaths during their active addiction may see these behaviors disappear in sobriety. In fact, any set of psychiatric symptoms or an apparent personality disorder could result strictly as a by-product of chemical addiction and could disappear altogether in sobriety. The only way to determine to what extent psychological/psychiatric symptoms exist apart from the chemical dependency is to see whether they diminish and disappear with sobriety.

12-Step Programs in Early Recovery

AA and other 12-step fellowship programs (founded on the basis of AA) are an exceptionally important part of the early recovery for CDs. For an estimated 10 million individuals who have found their recovery in various 12-step programs (Hughes, 1994), these programs are the single most important element of recovery. For newly recovering persons who are often dealing with guilt and shame and feeling isolated and unique, finding others who have gone through the same ordeal and appear to be happy and hopeful results in a powerful sense of affirmation and acceptance. To know that they are not alone and to have meetings and other members available at all times are forceful complements to formal therapy.

Most successful therapists require patients to attend appropriate 12-step meetings as a condition of therapy, usually on a therapeutic contract basis. This attendance may vary, depending on the frequency of other therapeutic activities. For example, if a therapist is seeing the patient twice a week, the patient may attend two or three AA meetings a week. Some therapists, when possible, want a new patient to attend 90 meetings in 90 days. For most individuals, 12-step programs play a much greater role than therapy in early recovery programs.[1]

[1]In the case of a CD with a compulsive behavior disorder, multiple fellowships, especially in early recovery, can overwhelm the person. Generally, it is wise to begin with AA and add other fellowships later.

Long-Term Recovery

The goal of long-term recovery is to help the client live a full and happy life in sobriety. These goals are really no different than they are with anyone else in therapy. The therapist, however, must be aware of the particular concerns of the CD, one of the most important being the fact that recovering individuals are much more likely than the general population to suffer from compulsive behaviors.

The time period involved in shifting from early to long-term recovery can vary dramatically from one individual to another. Time in early recovery can range from 6 months to 3 years, with most individuals making the shift sometime during the 6- to 18-month period. This does not mean that the addict or family must be in ongoing professional therapy throughout the period of early recovery. Brief (2 to 3 months) or intermittent therapy sessions during this time are adequate in many cases.

As the CD moves into long-term recovery, he or she is in need of more traditional therapy—be it individual, couples, or family therapy, or, as is most often the case, some combination of these. This stage of therapy focuses on issues related to family of origin, anxiety, depression, loneliness, marital conflict, lack of intimacy, codependent behavior patterns, and other difficulties in living.

The specific way the work proceeds is determined by the theoretical framework of the therapist. In most instances, the therapist is first concerned with addressing immediate symptoms such as anxiety and depression. Cognitive techniques, relaxation therapy, biofeedback, and hypnotic techniques can all be used to address these symptoms.

Next, the therapist should help the patient understand how his or her problems are a natural outcome of early life experiences. Early childhood work is very important in the treatment process for most CDs. It helps the patient deal with shame about feeling defective or feeling like a failure for being "so sick."

Patients often initially resist exploring early experiences for a number of reasons. First, resistance can result from an intuitive knowledge that the process is emotionally difficult. The therapist can recognize resistance when the patient begins to rationalize with statements such as, "The past is the past, and I want to move ahead" or "My parents did the best they could, and I have to accept responsibility for my own behavior."

Second, resistance can result from family rules. Family rules are unwritten and unspoken injunctions that define acceptable and unacceptable behavior in a family. Dysfunctional families often have rules that state that the family members should never question or examine each other's motives and behaviors, especially those of the parents. This prevents family members from realizing how parental treatment has affected them.

Finally, resistance can result from a sense of legitimate family loyalty based on the patient's fear that the therapist wants to condemn his or her parents. The therapist must be careful to respect the patient's fears. The therapist should let the patient know that although it would be helpful for him or her to understand his or her family, it is the patient's choice as to how much he or she wants to understand. When patients trust a therapist who takes time to assure them that the purpose is not to find fault with the parents but to understand how the parents' struggle to cope with the demands of their own lives and their own marriages may have affected the patients, resistance usually dissolves.

As the patient begins to develop a greater appreciation for the damage caused by growing up in a dysfunctional family, sadness and grief over his or her own lost childhood occur. There is also a sense of grief for the pain and suffering endured by the parents. It can be extremely beneficial for the patient to address some of these issues with the parents, but only if the patient feels confident that the parents would be receptive. Clients who anticipate defensiveness or rejection may not want to make themselves vulnerable. In instances in which one or both parents are deceased, a visit to the cemetery or writing a letter to the parents can be helpful.

Naturally, patients often begin to experience intense anger, either consciously or unconsciously, at parents during this process. These feelings, too, must be processed (i.e., experienced fully). At times, experiential "rage work" may be cathartic and helpful in getting in touch with these feelings. It is exceptionally important that a patient not undertake such work unless there is a commitment to ongoing therapy.

As clients more fully understand the past and are able to freely experience their emotional reactions to the past through whatever techniques the therapist employs, the clients become more serene and centered, and the symptoms begin to lessen. Patients find more awareness of their emotional experience and reaction to life. They enjoy life more, feel more capable of getting closer to others, experience a much greater capacity for joy, and feel less "pressured" by life.

Family and Couple Treatment

Chemical dependency is a family disease. At some time during the course of recovery, family therapy should be instituted. As a general rule, the sooner this begins, the better. The therapist must determine whether to begin family therapy with the couple alone or with the entire nuclear family. The preference is to begin family work with the couple only, unless one or more of the children are exhibiting troublesome behaviors or symptoms. After the marriage is stabilized, the children should be brought into family sessions.

Usually, members of a couple prefer to begin with individual therapy, especially if their level of trust with each other is low; however, couples should be encouraged to work together as soon as possible. The only exception is in the case of sexual addiction in which the recovering person has not yet been able to control his or her acting out or been able to end an addictive relationship.

Couples in a recovery process discover whether their relationship can work in a way that enables each of them to grow to the fullest extent possible. Although all couples get married for a combination of healthy and unhealthy reasons, couples in recovery probably have a higher proportion of unhealthy reasons (e.g., insecurity, escape from the family of origin) than do most other couples. That does not mean that they cannot have excellent marriages. However, at the beginning of recovery, they often cannot be sure what kind of marriage they can have. In spite of a strong commitment, people cannot simply "decide" to have a good marriage. They can only decide that they will work on discovering who they really are and what they need in a relationship to be fulfilled. They also discover whether they can have that kind of relationship with each other, assuming they are willing to expend a certain degree of time and energy.

There are three components to a truly healthy marriage. First, a couple must be able to work together to run a household and family. Second, they must be able to have an intimate and passionate friendship. Finally, they must be able to be lovers, that is, to share a romantic relationship. Without all three of these components, the marriage is incomplete.

The ability to work together to run a household requires similar attitudes (or a willingness to compromise) toward money, household cleanliness, childrearing practices, and so forth. This is usually not a major stumbling block for most couples, although one does occasionally hear, "We loved each other, but we just couldn't live together."

The centerpiece in any healthy relationship is the capacity to be emotionally intimate—to care passionately[2] about each other and to be continually moving in the direction of ever-greater intimacy and passion. This means that a couple should ideally have no important parts of themselves that they feel they must hold back from each other. In a truly intimate relationship, individuals decide to search their own souls and invite their partners to hold a spotlight so they can each see into the dark corners.

Intimacy does not just happen once and for all. A couple must actively strive to maintain it as each grows and changes over time. Couples must make the time to be together, with no distractions from children, telephones, or anything else. They must do this two, three, or four times a week. This enables them to "think out loud," to air any grievances, to express any displeasures, to share concerns and worries, to talk about dreams for the future, to share insights about life or information that is in any way important to them. True intimacy in marriage prevents the kind of "drifting apart" that always precedes more serious problems in a marriage.

Unfortunately, the demands of a busy life often make it difficult for a couple to find the time to do what is necessary to experience intimacy.Unfortunately, few couples make a serious effort to find time for each other.

---

[2]In this context, the word *passion* has little to do with sex. It is used to differentiate the level of even-tempered intimacy between two friends from that high-energy intimacy that hopefully exists between husband and wife.

The final component of a successful marriage is romance, which adds spice to the recipe of marriage. By its nature, it can occur only sporadically because it is "magic," and magic is only for special occasions. For some couples, romance is a weekend away. For others it may be dinner and a night of dancing, and yet for others, it may be a picnic in the countryside. Naturally, healthy romance has a strong erotic component and usually includes sex. Most couples who are happy in their marriage have a healthy romantic relationship.

Children in Chemically Dependent Families

It is almost impossible for a child to grow up in a chemically dependent family without being damaged. The damage may be extreme or relatively mild. The source of the damage may be very obvious, as in the case of overt physical, sexual, and/or emotional abuse, or it may be much more subtle as in the case of families who "look good" but show distortions in their communication patterns as a result of the need to hide and deny the chaos of chemical dependency.

As discussed at some length in chapter 4, anything that disturbs the healthy attachment ties between a child and the parental figures results in later psychological and emotional disturbances (e.g., anxious attachment, compulsive caregiving, reduced capacity for attachment). A child must have primary attachment figures available to respond to normal and healthy needs on a regular and consistent basis.

Considering chemically dependent families, in the more extreme cases (i.e., those typical of most SSCD and some HACD families), chaos reigns and the children cannot receive consistency or predictability in their lives or in the availability of nurturing caretakers. In fact, they are often physically abused and almost always emotionally abused. These individuals are likely to experience tremendous shame and feelings of rejection, which are quickly repressed because the children have no way of coping with them. According to Bowlby, such children are likely to detach from their affectional need system to a varying extent, depending on the emotional makeup of the individual and the severity and chronicity of the situation. If the detachment is extreme, a schizoid personality disorder may develop. In less extreme cases, the bullying type of codependent discussed in chapter 4 may result. Given a genetic predisposition, chemical dependency is very likely.

In moderately disturbed, chemically dependent families, children usually are subjected to a combination of emotional abuse and neglect. Such children are likely to suffer from various degrees of anxious attachment and/or compulsive caregiving. They also experience shame, but their shame is not quite as overwhelming and thus does not become as readily unconscious as that of the children from more extremely abusive families. They are more prone to anxiety than are children from more dysfunctional families because their environment is not consistently chaotic and destructive. They never quite know what to expect and, thus, experience high levels of free-floating anxiety. Children from families that are the least disturbed, are in some ways, at a greater disadvantage than those from more obviously dysfunctional families because they often have no conscious awareness that anything is wrong. The addicted parents are usually functional in many ways, holding respectable jobs and places in the community. Use of alcohol and other drugs may be more limited (e.g., evening cocktails, weekend binges). Rarely are the parents physically abusive, and their emotional abuse is generally more subtle. The greatest damage results from neglect. Parents cannot be emotionally available to their children or emotionally responsive to their needs if they are even partially intoxicated. The fact that the parents are physically present can even be more confusing, especially to a young child who can sense that the parents "are there but not there." Children from these families grow up feeling anxious, unhappy, and depressed and have no idea how their family situation contributed to these feelings.

Naturally, children who grow up under these various scenarios are not only neglected and abused themselves, but often witness many abusive patterns among other family members and rarely see healthy expressions of intimacy. There are often serious disturbances in communication patterns. These disturbances can lead to interpersonal difficulties resulting from an inability to communicate directly. Last, many family secrets and rules discourage members from discussing how they feel or how the behavior of one affects the other members.

These children enter adulthood lacking many of the skills needed to establish mature and caring relationships with others. The most difficult part for adult children of chemically dependent families trying to establish themselves in an adult world is that they unconsciously seek relationships that are at least familiar and known, namely, partners from similar backgrounds who do not put normal pressures on them for intimacy.

Sex and Romance Addiction

Because sex and romance addictions[3] are the most frequent form of compulsive behavior with CDs and because they are particularly destructive to marriages and family life, it is important to discuss the issue in some detail. The recovering CD who is also a sex and romance addict has to deal with two forms of

[3]The terms *sex and love addiction* and *sex and relationship addiction* are partly misnomers that have resulted in a certain degree of confusion. A more appropriate term is *sex and romance addiction.* The term *romance* is more specific than the term *love* and more clearly describes the phenomenon. In addition, the term *romance addiction* is preferred over *relationship addiction* because it allows one to distinguish individuals who are true addicts from those codependent individuals who continually get enmeshed in destructive relationships but whose motivation is not erotic as it is for the romance addict.

withdrawal at the same time, each one contributing toward feelings of loneliness, frustration, and anxiety. Moreover, the additional shame that accompanies feelings of weakness and immorality that result from a sexual addiction reinforces the CD's negative self-concept, which makes it more difficult to break the chemical addictive cycle and makes the person even more vulnerable to further sexual and romantic involvement.

It is important for the therapist to understand and counsel the patient that withdrawal does not end until all sexual acting out ends. For example, some patients' primary concern may be having affairs, and they stop having affairs. If, however, whenever they experience discomfort, they engage in pornography, masturbation, fantasy, or other forms of their sexual compulsion, they might experience withdrawal for years. Unfortunately, withdrawal from sexual addiction is very painful, and this pattern of prolonged withdrawal is not unusual.

The most common forms of sex and romance addiction are sexual fantasy, masturbation, sexually oriented massage parlors, pornography, and heterosexual affairs. Somewhat less common are homosexual affairs and involvement with various forms of prostitution. Some forms of sexual addiction can include rape, pedophilia, fetishes, and other serious and sometimes criminal behavior. Although these behaviors are compulsive, they include certain dimensions that are beyond the scope of this discussion.

In treating a sex and romance addiction, the nature of the problems involved in recovery depends in large part on whether or not the person is involved in a committed relationship. The single, uncommitted patient must ultimately decide what is acceptable dating and sexual behavior. Whereas some individuals choose celibacy until they are ready to make a solid commitment, the majority do not adhere to such a stringent criterion. Unfortunately, in these cases, many individuals judge themselves "cured" and jump into what they think is a committed relationship before they are ready. Although a certain degree of flexibility is necessary, the "1-year rule" is probably advisable in most cases: recovering CDs, especially those who are also dealing with a sex and romance addiction, should not even entertain the idea of a committed relationship until they are sober and clean for 1 year.

For single sex and romance addicts who do not choose to remain celibate, the best guideline is to avoid becoming sexually involved until a meaningful friendship has begun to develop. Naturally, this takes time and thus prevents the recovering person from moving too quickly. It also forces the addict to begin to deal with the fear of being vulnerable to another person. Addicts have always used sex and romance to protect and insulate themselves from others. Because of their fear of intimacy and vulnerability, they choose the "pseudointimacy" of sex and romance, staying high, and hiding their true selves. In recovery, they must give up this strategy and begin to attempt to become truly intimate. They must start to let themselves be known to another. It is not possible to do this unless they have begun to develop the kind of trust that cannot exist until after a friendship develops.

For recovering sex and romance addicts who are married or in a committed relationship, the problems involved are very different. In working with these sex and romance addicts, the therapist must first determine the patients' attitude toward their marriage or relationship and their sexual acting out. Many times, sex and romance addicts have developed a very negative image of the partner's sexuality and justify the behavior on that basis. They often have an ideal concept of what life would be like with someone else. The therapist has to help such clients see the delusion, rationalization, and denial involved in this thinking and help them recognize that although there may be real deficiencies in the sexual relationship with the partner, this is not the real reason for the sexual acting out.

One of the most difficult aspects of treatment for the sex and romance addict is the extent and timing of the sharing of the facts of the sexual addiction with the spouse. The ideal is for the client to tell the spouse the truth as soon as possible; however, in most instances, it is not wise for the patient to share this information until there is a period of sobriety and until the partner is involved in a recovery program (e.g., Alanon, therapy). It is best if the addict discusses this in the context of marital counseling, thus placing it in the context of developing the marriage.

In many instances, the partner has a fairly good idea of what has been going on, especially when the addict has been involved in affairs, but has never addressed the issue directly. This may have been because of the fear of having to deal with the truth, a feeling of superiority and control experienced by knowing that the partner felt guilty, or a willingness to allow it to go on because it permitted avoidance of having to deal with the partner's sexual needs. In some instances, the partner has been in total denial of the addict's acting out and feels a mixture of emotional betrayal and sexual inadequacy. The partner who suffers from very low self-esteem and chronic shame has a dominant response of a sense of sexual inadequacy and assumes that the sexual acting out is his or her fault. This usually results in the partner's initiating a frenzy of sexual activity that includes increased frequency and considerable experimentation. This behavior is based on the false belief that the solution to the problem lies in satisfying the sexual appetite of the addict so he or she will not act out again. It is the therapist's job to correct this false belief.

If a sense of betrayal is primary, the partner becomes extremely angry and withdraws emotionally and sexually from the addict. This reaction is more common and is a healthier response. In this instance, the therapist must educate the partner as to the nature of sex and romance addiction, emphasizing the fact that the addict's behavior was compulsive and was not a free choice. It must be made clear, however, that the therapist would understand if the partner decided to end the marriage because of the patient's infidelity. Sometimes there is too much pain and anger for the partner to deal with. Whatever the decision, the addict must understand and try to accept the feelings of the spouse. The wounds inflicted by a sense of betrayal take time to heal, and the addict must be patient.

In most instances, partners fluctuate back and forth between both reactions, with anger being primary. Although this is understandable, it results in even more confusion for the addict. It also requires understanding, flexibility, and patience by the therapist.

If the couple decides to stay together and work on the marriage, the therapist generally suggests that the couple have both individual and couple treatment plans. Individual treatment plans include individual or group therapy or both, attendance at separate 12-step meetings and getting 12-step sponsors. The couple treatment plan includes couples therapy and daily quiet time to discuss feelings and issues. Some therapists recommend a period of time (3 to 6 months) without a sexual relationship. This can be a time for the couple to get to know each other without the pressure and powerful emotions of sex.

During this time, although the addict is working on early recovery, the partner must see what part he or she played in this addiction and what the motives were. The partner must also accept a share of the responsibility for permitting the relationship to continue with an absence of emotional intimacy that allowed affairs to occur.

In some instances, the client may insist that the partner not be told about the sex and love addiction because of fear that this disclosure would mean the end of the marriage. Although these fears are often exaggerated, ultimately it is the client's responsibility to determine if and when this information is to be shared with the spouse. The therapist can only demand that the client not be acting out on an ongoing basis while pretending to work on the marriage.

12-Step Programs in Long-Term Recovery

The role of AA and other 12-step programs in long-term recovery is different from what it is in early recovery. In early recovery, as in early professional therapy, the goal is to support the individual to stay abstinent and provide help for emotional withdrawal.[4] The goal of the fellowships in long-term recovery is to enable the recovering addict to live life according to the philosophy embedded in the 12 steps. These steps remind people that they are addicts, teach them to cope with life's frustrations while maintaining serenity, and direct them to support others in the program.

There are a number of concluding issues that the addict and the family must deal with in long-term recovery. First, the addict is always an addict. Although some would prefer to "get past that" and forget that part of their lives, experience teaches members that those who forget, stop attending meetings, get back into the world of rationalization and denial, and end up relapsing. As with patients with other long-term chronic illnesses, recovery requires a daily and weekly regimen (a program) of beliefs, attitudes, and actions.

---

[4]In this context, emotional withdrawal refers to the period of time when the individual is learning to live and not pick up a drink or other drug. The addict's answer to day-to-day frustrations while in active addiction is to take a drink or other drug. In recovery, the person has other tools to rely on (e.g., calling a sponsor, going to a meeting).

Second, the person has to accept that getting sober does not solve life's problems. Members of the fellowship, however, can teach a person how to deal with day-to-day problems without picking up a drink or drug. There are many examples of individuals in the fellowship who have gotten sober only to have their lives fall apart (e.g., divorces, deaths in the family, lost jobs). The ones who stayed sober had a solid commitment to their recovery, worked an active recovery program, and utilized the program and members of the program extensively during those times.

Third, the goal of recovery is to quit fighting the next drink or drug and to live life to the fullest. If recovering persons had to live the rest of their lives miserable and frustrated, then the fellowship would not have much to offer. But the program can promise a life of opportunity and possibilities. For the first time, the person has a choice about how to live his or her life. In many ways, the individual stopped growing when he or she picked up the first chemical. In recovery, the emotional richness, serenity, and satisfaction of growth are experienced for the first time.

Fourth, one of the deepest satisfactions and most therapeutic events is for the recovering person to reach out to a struggling person and offer support, advice, and direction. This is the foundation of all 12-step fellowship programs and is what has catapulted them into a national phenomenon.

Finally, in the case of a CD with multiple compulsive behaviors, the individual must decide what fellowships to attend on a long-term basis. It is not unusual for the CD to suffer two to five compulsive behaviors that will differ in their chronicity, seriousness, and consequences. Experience teaches that the person must establish priorities based on the seriousness of the behavior and integrate multiple 12-step meetings. For example, a sex and romance addict or gambling addict may well have to attend both related compulsive behavior fellowships and AA. Generally, as time goes on, most successful recovering addicts with compulsive behaviors attend a chemical dependency 12-step fellowship and one or two other programs.

Myths of Treatment

The presence of compulsive behaviors adds a serious degree of complexity to the therapeutic enterprise. Unfortunately, a number of myths related to the issue of compulsive behaviors are all too common in the chemical dependency treatment community.

Myth 1 is that compulsive behaviors seen during active chemical dependency are merely a part of the addiction and are not a problem in recovery. Although many dangerous and unhealthy behaviors disappear in recovery, research and clinical experience strongly indicates that this is rarely true for compulsive behaviors. A good clinical history usually reveals that most of these behaviors actually preceded the chemical dependency. In fact, in some instances, as the person struggled to obtain alcohol and other drugs, compulsive behaviors actually diminished and became less severe. Thus, after the individual stops using chemicals, the compulsive behavior may actually be stronger than before.

If this possibility is not explored by the therapist and patient, the person is at greater risk to act out compulsive behaviors in recovery, and the ensuing emotional turmoil may well result in chemical relapse.

Myth 2 asserts that newly recovering individuals have an "addictive" or "compulsive personality" and must be aware that they are prone to substitute compulsive behaviors for their chemicals. This fiction denies the fact that the compulsive behaviors have a life (a biochemical and emotional process) of their own and are not simply a by-product of another process or merely a replacement for chemicals. This myth can result in the therapist and recovering person underestimating the strength of already existing compulsive behaviors and allow the patient to stay in a state of denial regarding them. Such an attitude can readily lead to relapse.

Myth 3, alluded to earlier, states that the treatment plan for the first year is not to drink, to go to 12-step meetings, and focus in therapy only on recovery from chemicals. Other issues should be dealt with later. As discussed previously, although there is a degree of validity to this approach for many recovering persons, it can be a very risky strategy for patients suffering from compulsive behaviors because it denies the high relapse potential if active compulsive behaviors are not addressed. The same is true for individuals suffering from severe codependency or other emotional problems.

Myth 4 states that, in recovery, the individual must change all behaviors that were in any way associated with the addiction—"people, places, and things." Again, although there is some validity to this belief, in many instances it fails to take into account legitimate personality and social needs of many recovering persons.

For example, SSCDs must find healthy ways to satisfy their needs for stimulation and novelty because these needs are based on biological processes and will not go away. One recovering SSCD still found skiing an exhilarating pastime, even though it was previously associated with chemical use. In recovery, the patient found sober friends who loved to ski and continued this activity. For the SSCD in recovery, behaviors and activities that are exhilarating and exciting are an important part of relapse prevention.

Likewise, the HACD in recovery must find ways to deal with high-anxiety levels. If a particular HACD was somewhat of a loner and found solace in reading, gardening, or other activities during addiction, the therapist may be afraid that any withdrawal is a sign of a "dry drunk" or unhealthy behavior. As in the case of the SSCD, however, these activities, as long as they are balanced, are important in relapse prevention.

Unfortunately, therapists have often failed to appreciate many of the different needs of the SSCD and HACD and, instead, have treated any activity in the addiction as though it were an unhealthy component of chemical dependency. Obviously, a therapist wants the recovering persons to achieve balance in their lives, with family, vocational, social, and personal areas contributing to the quality of recovery.

Types of Chemical Dependency and Relative Frequency

Cloninger, Bowman, and Sigvardsson (1981) found that approximately 25% of CDs in a general population were of the SSCD type and that 75% were of the HACD type. In residential treatment settings, however, those percentages are reversed—75% are SSCDs, and 25% are HACDs.

This difference probably results from the fact that SSCDs have more severe social, legal, health, employment, and financial problems and are therefore more likely to meet the behavior-oriented diagnostic criteria for severe chemical dependency and be recommended for more intense treatment settings. On the other hand, HACDs are more likely to be diagnosed as less severe and referred to outpatient treatment.

What about the uncomplicated "garden variety" alcoholics—those individuals who are neither SSCD or HACD and who apparently have no underlying neurotransmitter imbalance? These individuals stop drinking, go to 12-step meetings, and appear happy and symptom-free in sobriety. Unfortunately, not much is known about these individuals, either because they exist in such small numbers (as some professionals would argue) or because they do not appear in rehabilitation or therapy.

Although no one can be certain, it is reasonable to assume that these individuals do exist but that they have become an increasingly smaller proportion of the CD population over the years. Although the proportion of the CD population that is SSCD has remained relatively constant due to the powerful genetic factor involved in this type of dependence, current clinical evidence suggests that the proportion of HACDs has increased dramatically. This results from the greater number of people who use chemicals to cope with the ever increasing stresses of modern life. Thus, there are many more CDs overall and the majority of this increase is composed of HACDs.[5] Naturally, the number and proportion of CDs with compulsive behaviors have increased significantly as the proportion of uncomplicated CDs without compulsive behaviors has decreased.

Sex Differences and Compulsive Behaviors

Workers in the fields of mental health and chemical dependency must be aware of and sensitive to the different patterns of behaviors that are likely to be

[5]The great majority of early AA members were of the SSCD type, which would explain the extreme types of alcoholic behavior that first appeared in the AA "Big Book." It is interesting to speculate how AA would be different if the majority of the early members were HACDs.

displayed by men and women. This is also true when looking at compulsive behaviors.

Although female SSCDs do exist, the majority are males. As noted earlier, the compulsive behaviors that occur most commonly among male and female SSCDs are sex and romance, gambling, and stealing, with sex and romance being the most common. Unlike males, however, female SSCDs do not generally use prostitutes or massage parlors, become preoccupied with pornography, or become involved with multiple, concurrent affairs. Instead, they are more likely to engage in consecutive sexual affairs or compulsive masturbation.

In addition, many female SSCDs are involved in behaviors generally associated with the HACD, such as excessive shopping and spending, overexercising, and eating disorders; however, they engage in these activities not because they reduce anxiety, but because they are stimulating, resulting in a "high" (i.e., the runner's high, the overeater's high, and the shopper's high). Male SSCDs are unlikely to engage in these behaviors at all.

Among HACDs, there are proportionally more females than males, although the differences are not overwhelming. The male HACD generally suffers compulsive behaviors related to workaholism, overexercising, and eating disorders. Excessive shopping and spending also occur, although less so than for women HACDs. Finally, some male HACDs suffer from sexual compulsions, which are usually associated with SSCDs. Their behavior, however, generally does not include high-risk activities. Instead, their compulsive sexuality is generally limited to masturbation, pornography, and long-term sexual relationships. For these individuals, these activities serve to reduce their level of chronic anxiety.

The most common forms of compulsive behaviors among female HACDs are eating disorders and excessive shopping and spending. Compulsive exercise and workaholism occur, but are less common than for male HACDs. Female HACDs rarely show compulsive behaviors related to sex and romance. They may be involved in masturbation, fantasy, or a series of unhealthy relationships with men that have a sexual component. These relationships, however, are motivated primarily by strong codependent needs for attention and affection rather than sex. In many instances, the female HACD merely tolerates sex because it pleases men and is seen as a way to get attention.

One can probably best account for the different patterns of behavior between male and female HACDs and SSCDs on the basis of cultural factors and influences. For instance, in our culture, men are still the primary breadwinners, whereas women are typically the shoppers in the family. Thus, among HACDs, one would not be surprised to see work compulsions among men and shopping compulsions among women.

Accounting for the differences in the numbers of male and female SSCDs is more problematic. Cloninger suggested that femaleSSCDs were more likely to experience this type of alcoholism as psychosomatic illnesses rather than as novelty or risk-taking behaviors. Although cultural factors may play some role, the differences probably result from inherent biochemical factors (such as the tendency toward more aggressive activity in men) and only secondarily from cultural factors.

Although there are proportionally more female HACDs than male HACDs, this needs no further explanation because this difference is merely a statistical artifact resulting from the fact that a greater proportion of men, compared with women, are SSCDs, leaving relatively fewer men in the HACD category.

Summary

This chapter briefly addresses important principles, observations, and practices as they apply to CDs. Changing goals in therapy over time and some common, potentially dangerous myths regarding treatment and recovery that often result in increased likelihood of relapse are explored. Family, couple, and related general therapeutic issues are also examined. Finally, proper diagnosis, including the types of CDs as well as compulsive behaviors, complications, relative frequency, and sex differences are discussed.

The following chapters more fully describe the SSCD and the HACD and present important specific treatment and recovery considerations.

References

Cloninger, C. R., Bohman, M., & Sigvardsson, S. (1981). Inheritance of alcohol abuse: Cross-fostering analysis of alcoholic men. *Archives of General Psychiatry, 38,* 861–868.

Hearings before the United States Senate Committee on Labor and Human Resources, March 8, (1994) (testimony of Senator Harold E. Hughes, Ret.).

6

Sensation Seeker Chemical Dependents

SSCDs almost invariably come from families with generations of chemical dependency. In most, but not all cases, the father is alcoholic as well as overtly violent and abusive. Family life is often chaotic and characterized by fighting, discord, and a complete lack of order. There are often problems with the police and law enforcement agencies. In the schools, children of these families often receive special services from counselors, social workers, and special education departments. It should be reiterated that although this is the typical background for most SSCDs, some SSCDs come from more "normal-looking" families. Usually, however, closer examination reveals severe family dysfunction characterized by a lack of order that borders on chaos.

In discussing the sensation-seeking trait, it should be clearly understood that sensation seeking, in and of itself, is not a negative characteristic. Only when sensation seeking is combined with dysfunctional psychological development and destructive disorders such as chemical dependency and compulsive behaviors do we find such an extremely chaotic and destructive lifestyle.

The sensation seeker (SS) without chemical dependency thrives on excitement and risk-taking. When channeled into productive pursuits, sensation seekers are highly focused individuals who, in terms of careers, are most likely found in high-level positions in professions such as trial law and medical surgery, or they may be entrepreneurs running their own companies. They generally avoid bureaucratic and other relatively safe and secure but unchallenging positions. In recreational pursuits, sensation seekers are most likely to pursue risk-taking activities resulting in adrenaline rushes such as skiing, sky-diving, mountain climbing, and race car driving. Many sensation seekers however, fulfill their need for excitement or novelty by involvement in less physical and more intellectual or artistic pursuits (e.g., music, art, writing).

The typical SSCD begins using chemicals at an early age. Many begin as early as 12 and 13, with the great majority starting before age 20. SSCDs often report that when they took their first drink or used their first chemical, they felt immediate psychological and physical gratification and relief. They felt "normal" for the first time in their lives. As a result, SSCDs do not go through an extended period of social or recreational use that later progresses into a severe addiction. Instead, they use chemicals abusively right from the beginning, almost always getting intoxicated whenever they use. This pattern accelerates very quickly, and within 1 or 2 years, they develop a full-blown dependency on chemicals.

SSCDs are likely to abuse alcohol as well as a number of illegal drugs. Although they usually prefer stimulant drugs ("uppers") such as cocaine and amphetamines, they also abuse other types of drugs (sedatives, opiates, hallucinogens, etc.) if these are more readily available. SSCDs seem intent on altering their moods and changing their perceptions of reality and use almost any chemical means to achieve that end.

When SSCDs use chemicals and become intoxicated, they lose control of themselves to a much greater extent than do other people who may be equally intoxicated. They become extremely impulsive and use very poor judgment. Almost from the moment they pick up their first chemical, they undergo a radical transformation in their outlook and behavior.

Their impulsivity and lack of control often result in their acting out in antisocial ways, such as becoming assaultive, driving recklessly, and dealing in drugs. These behaviors increase the likelihood of arrest and a resulting criminal record.

The lifestyle of SSCDs gets out of control in a very short time. Medical, psychological, social, and legal problems abound. Despite these, SSCDs continue to drink and are usually fully dependent by their early 20s. They are often forced into treatment by legal authorities, and their numbers are probably overrepresented in rehabilitation and public clinics. Unfortunately, they usually are in deep and rigid denial and have little desire to change, at first. Thus, they usually have multiple treatment experiences by their 30s.

The SSCD and Compulsive Behaviors

Because SSCDs are continually seeking excitement, they are very likely to engage in compulsive behaviors that are risk-taking, active, and adrenaline-producing. Compulsive behaviors related to sex and relationships, followed by gambling and stealing, are the most common.

SSCDs likely suffer from more than one compulsive behavior and sometimes engage in as many as four or five, either consecutively or concurrently. They also may experience different compulsive behaviors or different forms of the behaviors at different times in their lives. For example, the child may steal compulsively but later become a sex addict. An adolescent may be a compulsive masturbator but later become involved in multiple affairs. A young man may gamble on horses and, in middle age, gamble on the stock market.

Case Study: Jack

Jack illustrates the typical SSCD. Jack was born into a chemically dependent family. His father was an alcoholic, and his mother was extremely dependent on prescription drugs. His life was spent waiting for the next disaster: his father's next drunk driving charge, his mother's next depression episode, or a sleepless night during one of his parents' marathon arguing bouts.

Jack remembers very little of his childhood before the age of 13. Most information about his early life comes through family stories and anecdotes. Because of the constant threat of chaos and conflict in his life that resulted from the ravages of parental chemical addiction, Jack made a pledge not to drink or take other drugs.

During his early teens, Jack discovered a number of things that served as an escape from the emotional chaos and isolation in his family life. He found a fantasy world in sexy detective novels as well as a new and exciting world in the streets. There he found boys to whom he could readily relate, boys who came from families much like his own. Although these boys rarely talked about their families or compared notes, they seemed to sense their common family experience and automatically gravitated to one another like true soul mates. Although it would be difficult to characterize their interaction with one another as "loving," there were definite emotional ties of caring and respect among these boys.

These teenagers were daring and reckless and cared little for the property or feelings of others outside their small clique. They developed a gang mentality in which daring and physical courage defined status in the group. That was all that really mattered. Jack discovered the thrill of stealing and of sexual conquests.

The boys took their first drink together (two six-packs stolen from a parked car), and each had that wonderful experience that accompanies that first chemical "high." From that day forward, their lives would never be the same. Getting high on alcohol, behaving recklessly, and having sex became the most important pursuits in their lives, consuming most of their time and energy.

Jack seldom experienced a negative feeling other than anger, and he was angry at everything. He countered other negative feelings such as anxiety and depression with anger, risk-taking, drinking, and sexual conquests. He avoided feelings of low self-esteem by actively seeking status and recognition within the group. Unfortunately, the group reinforced these antisocial attitudes by rewarding illegal, destructive, and criminal behavior such as stealing, vandalism, and sexual acting out. Fortunately for Jack, he was arrested only one time during these early years. Because of his behavior, he could have been arrested many times.

Both at home and on the street, Jack learned very quickly that there was a chemical for every problem and for every celebration. In addition, he learned that sex with any woman gave him something that no amount of alcohol could—a sense of being loved. Thus, chemicals and sexual acting out served as an antidote for every negative feeling or situation. The seeds of chemical dependency and compulsive behaviors were fertile and deep.

Jack left home immediately after graduating from high school. The next 6 years were very important to his development. Positive and negative motives began to compete within him. On one hand, positive forces made him want to make something of his life, to get married and settle down, to be the first one in his family to finish college, to be a professional, and to lead a respectable life. On the other hand, other forces compelled him to fight, drink and drug, sexually act out at every opportunity, and always disregard the other person. He was arrested four times during this period for various drunk and disorderly offenses.

Jack continued to live in a communal or ganglike environment, in which daring, fighting, sex, drinking, and drugs were valued, and he felt a part of something. At the same time, he became almost obsessed with the idea of becoming the first member of his family to graduate from college. He attended four different colleges over the next 8 years, usually transferring just ahead of being kicked out. At the same time, he was involved in an off-and-on relationship with a longtime high school sweetheart, who was a professional social worker. She became pregnant, and she and Jack were married. He was 24 and terrified of the responsibility that this move presented. He swore himself to fidelity in this marriage, but his chemical dependency and sexual compulsiveness were already firmly set, and his pledge did not last very long.

During the first 2 years of marriage, he became a father twice, graduated from college, and got a job as a counselor. He learned about alcoholism in counselor training, and after a number of disasters and near disasters, he experienced his moment of truth and began attending AA meetings. His denial and rationalization were very strong, and his initial sobriety was very difficult. He suffered a number of relapses but eventually maintained sobriety.

During these 2 years he also experienced a number of mature professional mentor relationships that reinforced positive work attitudes and rewarded achievement. He became quite responsible as a worker, father, and husband—except that his primary compulsive behavior was stronger than ever and he continued to act out sexually, having multiple affairs. This was Jack's life for the next 18 years.

Case Study: Sally

At first glance, our second SSCD example looks very different from a more typical SSCD, like Jack. Sally was not involved in antisocial behavior or chemical abuse at a young age and, in fact, lived a very "protected" life in her early years. As soon as the opportunity presented itself, however, a full-blown chemical dependency and compulsive pattern of behavior were evidenced.

Sally was a 35-year-old successful criminal attorney who had been married briefly and divorced. She had no children. She was an only child. Her early family life had been emotionally barren and empty. Her father was an angry and domineering man whose decisions were never to be questioned either by Sally or by her mother. Although never physically abusive, her father, if provoked, could be moody and volatile. At a young age, Sally learned to tiptoe gingerly around him. Her father was a successful medical surgeon and worked long hours; however, he kept close tabs on Sally's behavior and was extremely controlling and rigid.

Sally's mother was addicted to alcohol and prescription drugs. She drank secretly—mostly in her room—and neighbors and acquaintances were probably unaware of her dependency. Within the family, no one ever mentioned her mother's drinking. Teachers liked Sally and found her easy to deal with.

At the age of 14, Sally discovered the world of sexual fantasy and masturbation. She began to compulsively read romance novels and was soon masturbating on an almost daily basis. Because of the many restrictions Sally's father placed on her behavior, she did not have the opportunity to experiment sexually or use chemicals while in high school. Although Sally's mother drank at home, she kept her liquor supply hidden in her bedroom, and Sally just never thought of going to the trouble of sneaking in to steal her mother's liquor.

Her only early experience with alcohol occurred at age 15 when she went to a wedding with her parents. More out of curiosity than anything else, she drank alcohol for the first time. She discovered that she loved the taste as well as the sense of euphoria that it gave her and spent the rest of the evening sneaking drinks. She got very sick that night and vomited profusely, but somehow, her parents managed to stay unaware of her drunkenness and attributed her sickness to the flu. That was the only time Sally had an opportunity to drink until after college.

Sally's parents appeared to have no personal relationship whatsoever. They slept in separate bedrooms for as long as Sally could remember. They appeared to maintain a distant but polite relationship.

Sally never questioned her mother's drinking, which did not seem to visibly affect her. She became a very independent and self-contained child and was extremely efficient at taking care of herself from a very young age.

In school, Sally functioned well academically. Although not a brilliant student, she was very capable. Teachers liked her and she got along well with other children, although she remained somewhat aloof and never had best friends.

During her adolescent years, whenever Sally felt angry, anxious, or bored or began to have any other strong feelings, she would retreat into her world of sexual fantasy. Because she lived in a family that gave no recognition to feelings, she never learned to recognize or deal with her own feelings. If asked what her genuine feelings about something were, she would be unable to answer the question. She did not trust her own ability to feel, and at the first hint of any emotion, she would retreat into her world of sexual fantasy in which men loved and worshipped her.

After high school, Sally attended a small, conservative Christian college, primarily at the behest of her father. Because of the social culture, she was not exposed to alcohol, and the sexual mores on campus discouraged sexual activity except when couples were seriously involved in a relationship. Sally felt no desire for an intimate relationship and dated infrequently. Her sexual energy continued to be focused on romance novels and compulsive masturbating in the privacy of her room.

Sally did very well in college. She then attended a good law school and experienced a very real sense of pride in her accomplishments. In her second year of law school, she went out for drinks with one of her professors, ended up being seduced, and proceeded to have an intense 6-month sexual affair with this married man. Sally drank intensively whenever she was with her lover. Within a month after the termination of her affair, she found herself going out alone on weekends and picking up men at bars. She never brought the men home, but would spend the night and sometimes the whole weekend with them in hotel rooms, drinking and having sex. She never gave her phone number to anyone, and because she lived in a major metropolitan area, she had little trouble remaining anonymous. Sally continued her double life throughout the remainder of law school and for 3 years after graduation.

At that time, she began dating an attorney, and within a year they were married. When asked, Sally really had little idea as to why she married except that her husband was a nice guy and wanted to marry her, and it had seemed the right time to do so.

Sally, who prided herself on willpower, managed to restrict her drinking and gave up her weekend sexual forays. She was bored in her marriage, however, and continued to act out sexually with fantasy and masturbation. After about 1½ years, she began to drink again on the weekends and began her anonymous sexual adventures. She also began to use cocaine, which not only accentuated her sexual and chemical high, but also helped her to lose weight, which pleased her.

Naturally, Sally's husband was upset with her disappearing, and when she refused to seek counseling, he divorced her. Sally was neither pleased nor displeased with the divorce, although she did find it more convenient to be single.

Sally continued her double life with no apparent difficulties for another 3 years; however, she was finding it increasingly difficult to restrict her chemical use to weekends, and her binges got longer. Her colleagues soon began to notice. A number expressed their concerns to her about her appearance and work slippage. She denied that anything was wrong. One day, Sally collapsed at work, and after being taken to a hospital, she ended up in a chemical rehabilitation unit.

Although Jack and Sally appear very different at first glance, each of them demonstrates the defining characteristics of the SSCD. First, their chemical dependency became full-blown in a very short time rather than developing gradually and incrementally over time. Second, each of them engaged in very high-risk compulsive behaviors. Although Jack presents the more usual SSCD profile, Sally's case is interesting and enlightening because it was more atypical. Her behavior was not influenced by peers, and she did not travel in social circles that encouraged chemical use or sexual acting out. Moreover, although she might argue that she was exposed to her mother's drinking, there was no evidence to suggest that Sally was using her mother's liquor or that she was in any way exposed to any inappropriate sexuality as a child, other than her parents' seeming lack of sexuality. Once she drank, however, she drank excessively every time (binge drinking) and acted out sexually in a completely uncontrolled manner, exposing herself to numerous risks in the process. She, indeed, appeared to be an accident waiting to happen when she finally got the opportunity to act out. As stated a number of times earlier, this is typical for the SSCD and makes sense when one considers the biochemical factors underlying the behavior.

Biochemistry and Psychology of the SSCD

There is mounting evidence that the SSCD has differences in brain chemistry as compared with normals. For instance, there is some evidence that chemically dependent persons are different in their levels of endorphins, those natural, opiate-like chemicals that the brain produces which allow individuals to experience reward and tolerate pain. More substantial evidence exists to suggest that abnormalities in the neurotransmitters serotonin, dopamine, and norepinephrine exist in the SSCD (see chapter 3).

The most likely hypothesis is that the sensation seeker is born with an imbalance of these natural chemicals and that the behaviors they engage in and the chemicals they consume stimulate the brain pathways that are deficient, producing an intensity of mood change that is not readily understandable to those who do not have the imbalance. The activity or chemical allows them to feel "normal." In the case of alcohol, inhibitions are reduced, although in the case of cocaine and amphetamine drugs, which have particular appeal to the SSCD, stimulant effects compensate for the lack of natural chemicals. In addition, the pursuit of illegal drugs and illicit sex or also appeals to the SSCD because of the inherent excitement of risk-taking activities.

Thus, the situation of the SSCD is analogous to that of a diabetic who is underweight and eats a very bland diet. Under the circumstances, the symptoms of diabetes may not show. At some point, however, if the individual begins to use large amounts of sugar, diabetic symptoms appear. The disease was already there, waiting for the right circumstances to reveal itself.

Psychological Profile

Sensation seekers continually seek out novel situations to maximize the stimulation in their environment. Not only do they seek novelty, but they are particularly driven to novel situations with a high potential for risk. They find the unpredictable and the unconventional particularly appealing and often gravitate toward the unorthodox (fields such as religion and politics).

Interpersonally, SSCDs enjoy the company of others, in part, because other people are excellent resources for stimulation and excitement. They tend not to be particularly concerned about other people's thoughts and feelings and tend not to be particularly reflective about their own experiences.

While growing up, SSCDs are usually well liked and respected by their peers, although they rarely have close friendships. Academically, high SSCDs often perform poorly because many of them start getting into trouble at a young age; however, they often excel at one or two subjects that they find stimulating.

In psychiatric disorders, the high SSCDs are most likely to suffer from antisocial disorders followed by major depressive disorders and borderline personality disorders.

SSCD and Codependency

SSCDs do not demonstrate the behavioral traits that are typically associated with codependence, namely, excessive dependence on others, people-pleasing, anxiety, caretaking, and so forth. When we consider the less common type of codependence, however, which is related to Bowlby's "emotional detachment," we readily see the codependence inherent in SSCDs.

Both Jack and Sally came from homes in which they rarely, if ever, had their emotional and affectional needs met. Anxious codependents usually come from families in which there is at least some recognition of their needs—albeit on an inconsistent basis and in inappropriate ways. Emotionally detached codependents, however, usually have received no recognition whatsoever of their emotional needs. As a result, these individuals never have the experience of receiving any outside affirmation of their internal needs, which leads to confusion, frustration, shame, and self-hatred, most of which is unconscious. So, SSCDs adopt a strategy of compulsive self-reliance whereby they avoid anything even remotely approaching intimacy. Unlike the schizophrenic, who gives up entirely, the SSCD maintains the motivation to feel connected to the interpersonal world and so gets involved in a network of relationships based on some form of power, rather than on mutual respect and affection.

SSCDs have no reason to believe that anyone would have any genuine interest in them, so they attempt to control others with bullying and intimidation. In our examples, Jack engaged in a peer group in which relationships were defined by strength, daring, and power. Sally chose a profession in which she could readily assert power in confrontational settings, and her sexual acting out gave her a sense of power over men, whom she kept at an emotional distance.

Like the more typical people-pleasing codependents, bullying codependents are also plagued by deep-seated, unconscious shame. This results because, as children, their needs were unmet, and thus they assumed that they were defective. Their conscious awareness of their shame, though, is much more remote than it is for the people-pleaser. They maintain this lack of awareness by acting out almost continuously, never allowing themselves to be reflective for fear that they will be engulfed by feelings of dread and depression. They have no expectations that anyone will care about them, and so they have nothing to lose by turning their shame, insecurity, low self-esteem, and guilt into anger and striking out at the world.

Because of these various factors, recovery for the SSCD can be a very long and arduous road. Individual, group, and family therapy must be integrated with a solid 12-step recovery program, and, in some instances, antidepressant medication is indicated. In chapter 7, treatment and recovery are discussed at some length.

Summary

An accident waiting to happen is perhaps the best descriptive phrase for the SSCD. Genetics, biochemistry, and a dysfunctional family in which addiction often runs rampant combine to give SSCDs little or no chance to escape the ravages of addiction the moment they use any mood-altering chemicals or engage in any mood-altering behavior. Unlike the HACD, whose addiction develops slowly over time, the SSCD plunges headlong into addiction and chaos from the very beginning.

Because of their alienation from others, their lack of social skills resulting from an earlier onset of their addictions, their predisposition for serious depression, and the fact that they often come from an extremely dysfunctional family, their recovery is often complex and difficult. The next chapter deals with evaluation and treatment of the SSCD.

7

Sensation Seekers: Treatment and Recovery

Recognizing SSCDs is not difficult. As with skid-row alcoholics, the behaviors, characteristics, and attitudes of SSCDs are such that their identification is not the problem—what to do with them is the quandary.

The SSCD has a strong genetic predisposition to chemical dependency and a biochemical imbalance that results in the following:

1. High novelty seeking and risk-taking.
2. Low dependence on normal societal rewards.
3. Low harm avoidance, which further encourages risk-taking and novelty seeking.
4. A proclivity for multiple compulsive behaviors, most frequently inappropriate sex and relationships, gambling, and stealing.
5. Early and frequent chemical use and abuse and chemical-related problems before the age of 20.
6. Greater likelihood of a concomitant psychiatric disorder.

SSCDs are not model patients. Their hallmark is deep and rigid denial. They are not reliable and have a negative attitude toward authority. They are emotionally immature, insensitive to the thoughts and feelings of others, and oblivious to their own emotional state.

The PHQ is helpful in confirming a diagnosis as well as identifying dysfunctional issues (e.g., emotional relationship with parents, perception of physical and sexual abuse, chemical dependency in parents). The CBI is also extremely helpful because it determines the number and severity of past and current compulsive behaviors and the severity of chemical dependency.

The path to therapy for SSCDs almost always begins as a result of pressure from the significant people in their life because of acting-out behavior. They are more likely to enter treatment to satisfy the demands of family, legal authorities, or their employer than to accomplish any meaningful change. Thus, the therapist must begin by using the complaints and evidence presented by significant others in their lives to challenge SSCDs' denial.

When a therapist begins to have some success in reducing the level of denial, SSCDs are likely to begin to experience a surge of shame about their behavior. Although this is true for all SSCDs, it is especially true for female SSCDs. This occurs as a result of society's tendency to judge women more harshly than men for excessive chemical use and sexual acting out, which is the most typical compulsive behavior engaged in by SSCDs.

Perhaps the single most effective tool in helping SSCDs to cope with their growing awareness of shame is attendance at 12-step meetings. At these meetings, SSCDs have the opportunity to meet people in recovery who at one time acted out in similar ways. This kind of cxperience is the strongest possible antidote to shame. In addition, these meetings provide SSCDs in early recovery with a social network, sponsorship, and practical solutions to problems in living.

The psychiatric disorders of antisocial personality, major depression, and other disinhibitory disorders are the most common coexisting disorders among SSCDs. As noted earlier, accurate diagnosis in early recovery is extremely difficult. Separating the effects of chemical dependency and withdrawal from secondary psychiatric disorders presents many problems. When possible, it is best to defer final judgment until the individual has some time in sobriety, however, if psychiatric symptoms in early recovery are extreme, this necessitates a psychiatric consult at an early date, with possible use of medication and/or hospitalization, if necessary.

Compared with HACDs, most SSCDs generally are more difficult to treat successfully. Generally, their problems are greater in number and in seriousness. More extreme chemical dependency, the likelihood of a greater number of compulsive behaviors, more severely dysfunctional families of origin, less likelihood of a supportive social environment, and less likelihood of a regular job all result in a very guarded prognosis. Add to this their limited motivation to change their behavior and life through therapy and the outlook is not good.

In treating SSCDs, the therapist must often adopt the attitude of a member of a relay team in a long-distance race. SSCDs are generally in and out of treatment for a long time until they finally have experienced so much pain that they are ready to surrender. At times, the therapist is involved with an SSCD at an earlier stage of the process, whereas at other times, it is at a later stage of the process. Thus, the therapist must adjust expectations to the current stage of the process, always recognizing his or her own powerlessness in determining the ultimate destination of the patient.

If this discussion of SSCDs and the prognosis appears negative, the positive side is that once SSCDs have dealt with denial and other life problems, they can be quite successful in recovery. The same novelty seeking and adventurous spirit that plagued them for years with reckless and compulsive behaviors can be the basis of a commitment to recovery and self-exploration. In addition, they have a certain strength of character that, once pointed in the right direction, can be a powerful source of recovery. The problem is getting to that point.

Case Study: Jack

Jack, a recovering CD for a number of years, entered outpatient treatment after attending an Adult Children of Alcoholics (ACOA) residential program. He was pressured into ACOA treatment by his wife, Jane, who had experienced the same program and had entered outpatient treatment with a colleague. During the ACOA program, Jack got in touch with some very painful memories and experiences of his childhood. These included the pain of watching both addicted parents constantly fighting, his mother's numerous suicide attempts and hospitalizations, and the loneliness and isolation of his childhood. He remembered how his mother had made him feel very uncomfortable when she was intoxicated, crying, maudlin, and emotionally intrusive. He believed that he had never trusted a relationship (including his marital relationship) and that he was incapable of any close, intimate relationship. He had multiple affairs over the years, but did not deal with them in the ACOA program.

During the first outpatient session, which Jack had put off for more than 7 weeks following the ACOA treatment, he related that he had finally attended this session because he felt "strange, unmotivated, pained, and preoccupied." He kept thinking about the things that he had learned in the ACOA program, and he did not care about his day-to-day world.

During the first session, as Jack explored what had happened in the program and what it meant to him, he revealed to the therapist his numerous affairs during his marriage. Multiple sexual relationships and affairs were a pattern that went back to his midteens. The relationships were not serious commitments, and he made sure that he never got hurt. To Jack, words like *love, commitment,* and *fidelity* were hypothetical, nothing more than flowery words that poets and others used.

As Jack looked more closely at the relationships in his life, he felt that his children were the most important people in the world to him. For the first time, he had found a love that he could not explain away as some kind of game in which the partner was trying to get something from him.

Because the session was going well, and Jack seemed to trust what was happening, the therapist explained to Jack that he had the symptoms of a sex addiction and that he would have to deal with this. Jack was quite upset and threatened by this revelation. Because there were no Sex and Love Addiction

Anonymous (SLAA) meetings in the area, Jack could explore the issue further only during his therapy.

Over the next year with the therapist, Jack explored his sexual addiction, along with many issues relating to his childhood and how these events affected his life today. Unfortunately, Jack was not able to completely give up his sexual acting out. He struggled with one relationship in particular, a woman who worked with him. She seemed to be a sex addict also and had much the same pattern as Jack. With great difficulty, Jack finally ended the relationship. It troubled him, however, that he felt that deep inside, he was still struggling with his denial—that he had not fully accepted his powerlessness. In fact, he had not fully accepted the extent of the devastation that his sexual behavior had caused him and his family, and he had not accepted that he was out of control with his behavior. To accept the compulsiveness of his behavior would mean that he would have to work harder to give it up. In his unconscious, he preferred to hang on to his shame and guilt rather than to do whatever was necessary to change. In his world of delusion, if he was not a sex addict, then a relapse was not a terrible thing.

In the months that followed, he worked on his denial, his extreme withdrawal from his compulsive behavior, his periods of anxiety, his loneliness, and his low self-esteem. After 3 months, it became clear that it was time for Jack to tell his wife about his sex addiction. In a very tense session with Jane, Jack revealed that he was a sex addict and that he had had a number of affairs over the years. Although Jane was devastated by this revelation, she had clearly suspected it for a long time. In her own individual counseling sessions, Jane had to deal with this issue. Still, the actual confrontation was crushing for both of them. At this point in consultation with Jane's therapist, Jack and Jane entered couples therapy.

In couples therapy, it became obvious that both were committed to the relationship and to healing together. Obviously, they had many issues to deal with, trust being the most pressing. Over the following months, they spent time exploring this issue and giving Jane the opportunity to express her rage, resentments, and sense of betrayal. Jack did not reveal the specifics of his affairs, and it would not have benefited either of them for him to do so. There was a natural curiosity on Jane's part, but it would not have served a purpose for Jack to go into any of the details. In fact, it would have been counterproductive.

While Jack was out of town, Jane found a number of letters and pictures from his relationship with the woman at work. When Jack returned home, he was confronted by a spouse who was almost insane from reopened wounds and rage. During the confrontation and later in treatment, he could not explain the letters and pictures except to say that he was out of control. Although he had not continued the affair, he believed that he kept the material for a sense of security, to know that his addiction was still there if he needed it. This is similar to a recovering alcoholic keeping a fifth of whiskey in the cabinet. If he or she wants it, it is there; if the pain of withdrawal becomes too great, the alcoholic can always take out his or her addiction and ease the pain.

In exploring the issue further, it became obvious that Jack was defining his sexual addiction very narrowly. He wanted to believe that his addiction was the affairs. He did not want to give up his sexual addiction; he wanted to stop having affairs. He was afraid that affairs would cost him his marriage and that he might get a sexually transmitted disease, and he did not want the shame and guilt that he now experienced and that which would result from any additional affairs. He did not want, however, to give up pornography, flirting, sexual conversations (what he called the head games), or other aspects of the addiction. He believed that the pain of total withdrawal was more then he could deal with at that time.

This form of denial and the results caused him even greater pain. He now had to deal not only with the serious blow to his marriage, but also with the continuing active addiction. Although this incident was devastating for Jane, it was a major breakthrough for Jack. He knew and accepted without reservation that he was an addict and that he was out of control. He was ready to do anything to recover.

The situation was so desperate that it was suggested that Jack change jobs (which he did) and that both enter an 8-day residential couples program. Although Jane went with the purpose of ending the marriage, the excellent individual and couples work they experienced changed her mind. She discovered the extent of Jack's illness, the pain it was now causing him, and his commitment to their marriage. Individually and as a couple, they developed an aftercare plan.

On their return home, they immediately reentered couples therapy as part of their aftercare plan. They continued to work on trust, intimacy, coupleship, and day-to-day issues such as fighting fairly and communication.

Jack went through a serious and painful withdrawal experience. He suffered periods of depression and a lack of motivation. He questioned the purpose of life without the highs of compulsive sex. His whole life had been centered around his acting out. He fought the lingering and more difficult aspects of his compulsive sex (e.g., fantasy, masturbation, sexualizing women) and other consequences of withdrawal.

Jack started attending a number of newly formed SLAA meetings in the area. He asked a solid member of the SLAA group to be his sponsor. After 6 months of attending SLAA and additional counseling, Jack and Jane were doing well and were discharged.

Jack's case illustrates a number of important points. He was not experiencing a hypersexual drive. His affairs were more an effort to counteract a sense of abandonment and loneliness than the result of hypersexuality. He sexualized his feelings.

In addition, Jack did not suffer a secondary psychiatric disorder, although his emotional state during his early treatment and withdrawal may have been easily misdiagnosed as depression.

Also, Jack illustrates the intensity of the denial of SSCDs. Although he was quite articulate and could verbalize a high degree of understanding of the situation, he was not able to vigorously confront the compulsive behavior until the crisis of the letters and pictures, which he could not rationalize away. As with chemical dependency and any compulsive behavior, it generally takes a dramatic event to break through the denial. This is because of the deep pain the addicts face if they give up this defense. As soon as they start getting honest, the pain comes, and they step back into denial.

Case Study: Sally

Sally's case presented an interesting challenge to the therapist because, like most SSCDs, she does not have much conscious experience of feeling emotional discomfort in her life. Instead, she always acted out in various ways whenever negative feelings began to surface. Individuals like Sally can be difficult for many clinicians, given their training and clinical experience, which are more likely to have been with high-anxiety individuals, in which the pain and emotional discomfort is closer to the surface and easier to explore. SSCDs' propensities toward emotional denial is so deeply ingrained and they are so adept at it that therapists can be easily frustrated unless they realize that SSCDs are not trying to be incorrigible.

Sally entered treatment following a physical and emotional collapse at work, after excessive alcohol and other drug binges. Like most SSCDs, she was motivated to get out of a difficult situation, a threatening predicament, an ominous, job-threatening circumstance; she was not motivated for recovery. Sally, however, had the advantage of being very intelligent and of using her intellectual prowess in the challenge of figuring out her life. The therapist used this to her advantage by "educating" Sally about her life, how she was damaged in her early development, and how she tried to escape into chemicals and sexual behaviors. Because of her genetic makeup, she was almost immediately chemically addicted. Thus, although her emotional problems did not cause her addiction, they certainly led to her initial chemical use and acting out.

This kind of intellectual understanding is not particularly effective in promoting change in a patient's life, but it can be very important in laying the groundwork for therapy and developing a therapeutic alliance with the patient. Especially to an intelligent person, it is important that therapy make sense.

Early Recovery

In early recovery, the most important goal was for Sally to accept her chemical dependency and powerlessness over it. Although there was a possibility that Sally would not struggle with compulsive sexuality once she was free from chemicals, her history suggested otherwise. Her early escape into sexual fantasy preceded her chemical use and would probably continue into sobriety unless the problem was addressed.

The first issue that faced Sally's therapist was to help Sally deal with her shame about her acting out. Concerning her shame about alcohol abuse, the therapist readily pointed to Sally's mother's alcoholism and the fact that Sally's own history of chemical abuse suggested a high genetic component for her own alcoholism. Concerning her sexual behavior, the problem with shame was somewhat more difficult. There was no evidence that there was any sexual abuse in Sally's history, and although some might argue that sexual abuse can be subtle or covert and is always a precursor to sexual addiction, such an assertion has little, if any, hard evidence to support it. It is more likely that Sally's compulsive sexuality resulted from her natural sensation-seeking personality coupled with an oppressive, lonely, and emotionally barren early family life. It is also possible that there was a family history of sexual addiction.

For instance, in Sally's family, her parental grandmother abandoned her husband and 3-year-old child (Sally's father) and ran away with another man. Sally's grandfather remarried when her father was 5, and his stepmother was the only mother he really knew. Although Sally's father was never clear on the facts, he remembered hearing family members refer to his biological mother in negative terms such as "tramp" and "slut."

Although one can never be sure about family history and sexual addiction, Sally found some solace and relief in the possibility that there was sexual addiction in the family. It helped her to feel less ashamed and less immoral.

Perhaps the greatest antidote to shame is the recognition by individuals that they are truly powerless about their addiction. Their behavior is not volitional, but is under the control of psychological and emotional motivations determined, in part, by biochemical factors over which they have no control. Thus, they must "surrender" to their powerlessness and accept the reality of their addiction.

Early in recovery, intellectual realizations do not preclude struggles with compulsive sexuality. Like many sex addicts, Sally never had her emotional needs met. Rather than deal with the emotional pain associated with her sense of abandonment, she retreated to an area in which she was desirable, wanted, and even needed, an area in which she had power—her world of sexual fantasy and acting out. She sexualized her emotional needs.

Eventually, compulsive behaviors take on a life of their own and become functionally autonomous. They become quite distinct from those factors that originally contributed to their development. Thus, even as Sally dealt with the pain of her childhood, she needed to focus much attention on whatever tactics were necessary to avoid acting out sexually as she gradually came to terms with her emotional pain and loneliness.

Long-Term Recovery

In long-term recovery, Sally had numerous issues as she struggled to develop meaningful relationships, first with women and later with men. She attended both AA meetings and SLAA meetings. Luckily, in her area there were SLAA meetings attended by a number of other women (unfortunately, in many areas, SLAA is attended primarily by men).

The therapist helped Sally realize that she must take into account her natural sensation-seeking propensity. She had to look for healthy challenges in her life as she physically and emotionally withdrew from the adrenaline high that was associated with her sexual acting out. Without healthy behaviors, she was likely to relapse into unhealthy behaviors, especially sexual acting out. Sally developed a strong sense of recovery and health and became quite involved in competitive-league golf and racquetball, which she found stimulating, exhilarating, and challenging.

After a year of therapy and with a number of solid female and male friends, Sally was ready to date. Sally eventually became emotionally and sexually involved with a man from the AA program. She experienced feelings of confusion. For Sally, sex was usually divorced from sincere caring, and she did not know how to blend the two. She felt deeply vulnerable, powerless, and scared. She was encouraged to discuss these feelings with her partner and to go slowly.

Sally eventually was able to find comfort in this relationship and ended her therapy a few months later. Unfortunately, after a period of time, the relationship was broken off by her boyfriend. Initially, Sally felt devastated. Although she was not tempted to use chemicals, she did feel the urge to act out sexually. Instead of doing so, however, she returned to therapy and dealt with her feelings of hurt and abandonment. Never before had Sally confronted powerful feelings of hurt and abandonment without running from them and acting out, and this incident proved to be a significant catalyst in Sally's emotional growth.

Sally terminated her therapy after 3 months, feeling confident that with the help of the program and her friends she would be able to deal with whatever life had to offer her—both the good and the bad. As she herself said in her last therapy session, "Pain is inevitable, but misery is optional."

Summary

In this chapter we have examined the ideas and principles used in the treatment and recovery of SSCDs. The respective recoveries of two SSCDs were reported in detail. Although these individuals differed in many fundamental ways (e.g., one was a married man who came from an obviously chaotic family, had been chemical-free for a number of years, and was active in AA, whereas the other was a single women who was newly sober and who came from a family whose pathology was less obvious), they each shared the typical character traits of the SSCD.

Each of the patients entered treatment because of outside influences. Jack got into treatment at the behest of his wife, whereas Sally entered treatment after she collapsed at work. This is typical of SSCDs, who do not seek treatment because of intense psychological discomfort. Their denial is so powerful, and they are so well defended that they are completely out of touch with their own feelings.

Diagnosis of the SSCD is generally not difficult. Their early-onset chemical dependency, which rapidly progresses out of control; their chaotic lives; and their risk-taking and sensation-seeking behaviors make it very obvious that they are SSCDs. Naturally, the degree of psychological denial is directly proportional to their lack of identification as CDs and to the underlying unconscious shame. Because of their high degree of denial, SSCDs do not initially respond to traditional therapeutic approaches. Thus, as therapy progresses and their defenses begin to lessen, SSCDs are in danger of acting out or experiencing intense depression.

Although it is obvious that SSCDs must first stop using chemicals, it has not always been obvious that this is only the first step. Various sensation-seeking forms of compulsive behaviors do not disappear merely because of chemical abstinence. Our case example of Jack makes that perfectly clear. His marriage, his psychological growth, and his capacity for intimacy remained crippled for many years because he continued to be powerless in his sexual addiction (even though he was abstinent from chemicals and heavily involved in AA).

Compulsive sexual behavior, perhaps as no other compulsive behavior, causes as much difficulty, both practically and psychologically, for the recovering SSCD. Jack was forced to change jobs and almost lost his marriage. Sally lost her marriage, in part, because of her sexual compulsion. Both Jack and Sally experienced intense feelings of shame about their sexual behaviors. This is understandable, given traditional views of sexuality and morality in our culture.

Although these two cases did not include other compulsive disorders, gambling, stealing, and other forms of risk-taking behaviors are often found in SSCDs and are extremely destructive to the well-being of SSCDs and their families and can result in years of hardship. Thus, even when recovering SSCDs show no signs of gambling or stealing disorders, they should be educated to the possibility of (and propensity to exhibit) compulsive behaviors and be made aware of the warning signs.

Because of the degree of shame, it is not uncommon for the SSCD to experience serious depression sometime during recovery. This is compounded by the intense withdrawal (feeling lonely, vulnerable, unmotivated, nervous, and irritable) from sexual addiction that the SSCD also experiences. Although antidepressant medication should be used only if necessary, SSCDs may need antidepressants to prevent relapse or to avoid debilitating depression; however, mood-altering chemicals such as benzodiazepines are inappropriate.

Because of their propensity to be involved in a number of compulsive behaviors, long-term recovery for SSCDs generally includes a number of 12-step fellowships. At one time, one fellowship may be more prominent in an individual's life, whereas at another time, a different fellowship may be more important. If people live in an area in which there are no meetings for certain compulsive behaviors, then they could consider starting one or using their 12-step AA program to address their compulsive disorders.

Finally, SSCDs are born with an innate need for novelty and sensation seeking. Unfortunately, this sensation-seeking characteristic has traditionally been suspect among professionals, often being viewed as part of the addiction or a character defect that can trigger relapse. This bias has been counterproductive in treating SSCDs because it results in the failure to encourage them to find healthy outlets for their sensation-seeking needs. This may include the pursuit of professional challenges, entrepreneurial opportunities, and recreational or artistic activities. If SSCDs do not pursue these activities in sobriety, there is an increased chance of relapse, the development of another compulsive disorder, or a life of tedium and boredom.

8

High-Anxiety Chemical Dependents

The second type of addicted individual is the HACD. As a group, HACDs represent a much more widely divergent group than the SSCDs. HACDs' patterns of chemical abuse are more highly variable, as is the degree of their dependency.

The great majority of HACDs often go through their entire lives without ever coming to the attention of authorities because they do not typically get involved in criminal behavior or the street culture of drugs. Their drug of choice is usually alcohol. In fact, HACDs are often model citizens and can be found in every walk of life: laborers, educators, physicians, corporate executives, clergymen, and individuals at the highest levels of government. So-called functional alcoholics are typically the HACD type.

On the other hand, in the later stages, HACDs may be daily drinkers who cannot function at all either socially or vocationally. Some of them may even be derelicts living in the street.

HACDs typically begin to use chemicals on a regular basis after age 20 and, as mentioned, are more likely to use only alcohol. If other drugs are used, more than likely they are sedative types of prescription drugs or marijuana.

For the HACD, alcohol is usually used socially for a number of years before there are any obvious signs of dependence. Because of the regular use of alcohol after high school and the excessive use of alcohol on U.S. college campuses, it is extremely difficult to sort out potential HACDs from those who abuse alcohol as part of the accepted social scene. For certain CDs (generally, sensation seekers), there are early warning signs such as blackouts, drinking fast, and drinking alone. Many HACDs, however, do not show early warning signs, and only a number of years after college does it become easier to discriminate HACDs from normal social drinkers or casual drug abusers. For most people, consumption of alcohol and other drugs generally drops off markedly between age 25 and 30, although HACDs show an ever increasing tendency to use chemicals.

Although most HACDs begin abusing alcohol in their early 20s, not all do. It is not uncommon to find HACDs who do not begin drinking until much later in life, and they have fewer legal, occupational, marital, and social problems as a result. This is especially true for women. Unfortunately, this can make it easier for such individuals to maintain denial because they are quick to point out that they never picked up a drink until they were in their 30s or 40s and so could not possibly have a drinking problem! Obviously, to them, "real" alcoholics start drinking at a much younger age.

At a later point, an event or series of events may throw such persons into a state of crisis or trauma that leads to increased drinking or drug taking. This event may be the loss of a job, a divorce, the death of a loved one, or any kind of life event that throws them into a state of insecurity, inadequacy, or sense of abandonment. In their social drinking, they learned very well the stress-reducing qualities of alcohol and other drugs, and so, when experiencing intense emotional stress, it is easy for them to fall back on the chemical or chemicals that they have learned to trust over the years.

HACDs and Compulsive Behaviors

HACDs are less likely than sensation seekers to engage in compulsive behaviors, although the occurrence of compulsive behavior in this group is certainly much greater than in the population at large. When they do engage in compulsive behaviors, they are more likely than SSCDs to engage in only one, rather than multiple behaviors. Among HACDs, a compulsive behavior naturally serves the purpose of reducing anxiety. Thus, eating disorders, compulsive exercising, workaholism, and excessive shopping are common. Although sexual addiction also occurs, the particular behaviors are different from those typically seen among SSCDs. Although SSCDs usually engage in multiple affairs and other forms of risk-taking, sexual acting out, HACDs are more likely to engage in compulsive masturbation or unhealthy, long-term romantic affairs. Definitive diagnosis of compulsive behavior is difficult while the person is actively addicted to chemicals.[1] Although there is no unanimous agreement about the length of sobriety necessary before an accurate diagnosis can be made, it would seem that at least 3 months is the absolute minimum, although some time period closer to a year is preferable.

[1]This is because many individuals behave impulsively when using chemicals and thereby act out in any one of a number of ways (e.g., eating, sexually). When sober, however, they no longer act out. Truly compulsive individuals continue to act out when not using chemicals. In fact, the compulsive behavior often increases in sobriety.

Case Study: Jim

Jim is a 42-year-old successful accountant who came into therapy at the suggestion of his wife. Jim reported problems in concentrating, difficulties in sleeping, and excessive fear and insecurity concerning financial and professional concerns. Jim's wife, Kathy, reported that he is extremely impatient and short-tempered with her and their two teenage sons and that she is concerned about his excessive drinking.

Professionally, Jim is popular and well liked by his colleagues. They describe him as an extremely competent professional who has a reputation for being meticulous in the preparation of his work, often working well into the night a few evenings each week. On questioning, it was discovered that Jim is a weekend drinker. After work each Friday he goes to "happy hour" with some of his coworkers. Lately, he has been staying later at happy hour, often failing to come home until midnight. Jim usually resumes drinking on Saturday afternoons after completing his Saturday chores. He and his wife then go out to dinner with friends, and Jim continues to drink until well into the evening. On Sunday afternoons, Jim begins to drink once again and continues to drink until 6 or 7 p.m., at which point he stops until the next weekend. Jim never gets belligerent or sloppy when drinking. In fact, he and his wife report that he appears happy and relaxed whenever he drinks.

Both Jim and his wife feel they have a good marriage, although Kathy admits she would like to see Jim curb his drinking. Although he has never told Kathy, Jim admits to having had a number of relatively long-term affairs during their 20-year marriage, all with women with whom he has worked. In fact, Jim was still involved in his most recent affair when he began therapy. Jim never gave any serious thought to leaving his marriage, because he felt he loved his wife. Despite extreme anxiety, guilt, and shame over the affairs, he found that his involvement with women helped him to feel more secure and confident in his professional identity.

Jim was raised in an intact Roman Catholic family with two older sisters. His father was a working-class laborer who drank every weekend. In later years, he began to drink during the week. Jim had a very troubled relationship with his father. Although never physically abused, Jim was continually the recipient of emotional abuse from his father. Jim was extremely close to his mother, who died when he was 12 years old. Shortly after his mother's death, Jim began to display symptoms of depression and anxiety. He found it increasingly difficult to stay motivated academically, and his grades began to slip markedly. He no longer participated in extracurricular activities. He became withdrawn, socially isolated, and less confident and began to suffer from numerous minor illnesses. At age 16, Jim met and began to date his future wife, Kathy. Shortly thereafter he began to feel better about himself. His grades improved, and he became more socially outgoing and less worrisome. He eventually entered a local college, continued to date Kathy steadily, got married on graduation, and went to graduate school.

Jim began to drink socially in college. Although he never suffered blackouts and rarely got helplessly drunk, he often drank more than he had originally planned, he drank very quickly, and often he enjoyed drinking alone. He was always prone to strong hangovers, which made him feel extremely anxious and guilty, along with the usual physical symptoms. After college, Jim's drinking continued unabated.

Jim had stopped drinking 3 months before coming into therapy. He stopped drinking primarily because of concerns about his health and a desire to "get into shape." On questioning, Jim also admits that he has been developing a problem. Although he is not quite ready to call himself an alcoholic, Jim feels that he should not drink again because he began to see some parallels between his drinking and his father's. There are times on the weekend when Jim misses drinking, and he has found that it helps to "keep busy on the weekend."

Case Study: Liz

Liz was born into a chemically dependent family; both her mother and father were chemically dependent. The family looked like a typical middle-class family, with a father who was being a good provider and mother who appeared to be attentive andwho stayed home and raised the family.

Each evening, Liz's parents had cocktails, beginning at about 5 p.m. and continuing until 8 p.m. or later, when they finally ate dinner and then collapsed into bed. From about the age of 10, it became Liz's responsibility to care for her two younger brothers each evening. That meant feeding them, helping with homework, and getting them to bed while her parents "unwound" with cocktails.

Liz's parents both bragged to friends about her "maturity." In fact, Liz's mother observed that she herself was not as responsible as Liz and did not know how she would ever get along without her. There was much truth to that observation, because Liz's mother began to drink earlier in the day and rarely got the housework done. On weekends, Liz helped "catch up" around the house.

Liz and her father were overly close. He often referred to her as "little mother." Although there was never any overt sexual behavior, her father's behavior was often inappropriate, as on those evenings when he would get drunk and end up collapsing on Liz's bed with her. There was also a kind of "intensity" in her father's affection toward her that made Liz feel extremely uncomfortable. Moreover, she was ashamed of those feelings of discomfort because she could not explain them. Obviously, her father's intensity had strong sexual overtones that caused confusion for Liz as well as shame regarding her own sexuality and developing femininity. Moreover, because of the covert nature of her father's inappropriateness, Liz had no idea why she felt the way she did. She had no close friends, was a mediocre student, and took no part in school activities. She took little interest in her personal appearance and was pretty much unmotivated to do anything except "get by" academically. For the most part, she went unnoticed by teachers and other children. While maintaining a calm and drab exterior, Liz was consumed inside by shame, anxiety, and repressed rage. She slept little, overate, and became overweight. Taking care of her brothers and helping her mother were the only activities in her life that felt meaningful.

In the ninth grade, when she was 15 years old, a teacher took an interest in Liz, and for the first time, she did well in school. Her academic achievement that year set the pattern for many years to come. It helped her forget her shame. Books and learning became a comfortable escape, and the sense of achievement helped to fill the emptiness she felt at her core.

Liz continued to excel academically throughout high school, and she became involved in academically oriented school activities such as the debating society. She never dated. Being around boys made her feel shame and discomfort.

She was not interested in social activities and had no close friends, although other teens liked her because she was always willing to help others with their homework. She continued to experience excessive anxiety, focusing most of her worry on her mother's health and her younger brothers' welfare. She continued to suffer from sleep disturbance and lost weight. She ate only enough to allow her to function, always bothered by a "nervous stomach" condition as well as a concern about becoming overweight again.

At age 17, in her junior year of high school, Liz's father died suddenly from heart failure, and this magnified her shame. Throughout her life, Liz had always experienced a confusing ambivalence toward her father. Part of her loved him dearly, whereas another part of her was relieved by his death. This magnified her shame and resulted in her feeling that she was somehow responsible for his death.

Although she had an excellent academic record, Liz decided that she could not go to college because she needed to contribute financially to the family's welfare and had to care for her mother and two younger brothers, who were now in high school themselves. Her mother's drinking had progressed to the point that Liz had assumed all of her mother's household duties as well as the overseeing of her brothers. Liz also worked as an office manager at a nearby manufacturing firm. She was an excellent worker and earned a respectable salary, which, when combined with her father's insurance money, allowed her to support the family in a modest lifestyle.

As far as anyone knew, Liz had no relationships with men. In fact, however, she had a long-term relationship with a married man much older than herself who was an independent consultant doing business with the company. He lived in another part of the country but spent 2-week periods at Liz's company about six times a year. During these visits, Liz spent as much time with him as she could. Although the relationship included sex, that was not especially important to Liz. What was most important to Liz was that she was treated kindly and gently by her friend and felt a sense of security in knowing he was in her life.

This was true, even though she had no contact with him when he went home, and she knew he would never leave his marriage. Although her value system made her believe that the relationship was wrong, that made little difference to her when compared with the sense of security she received from it.

On graduation from high school, each of Liz's brothers went to the state college, graduated, and got married. Liz stayed at home and continued to care for her mother. She eventually began to drink and found something that all the achievement and caretaking could not provide, a quieting of the turmoil and abject feelings that threatened to engulf her. Gradually her drinking increased, but seldom to the point of obvious intoxication. She drank mostly in the privacy of her home or at necessary social functions.

Liz's mother continued to drink heavily, her health deteriorated, and eventually she died. Liz was 35 years old at the time. After her mother's death, Liz's own drinking escalated. Eventually, she was unable to sleep even with the help of alcohol, and so she started taking sleep medication under her doctor's advice. At the age of 37, she was arrested for drunk driving and ended up in treatment.

The Dynamics of the HACD

Jim and Liz represent two very different kinds of examples of the HACDs. Thousands of other variations exist in the real world, but, as diverse as each example is from the next, closer analysis reveals certain underlying commonalties.

Biochemical Profile

High anxiety individuals differ from other people across a wide variety of physiological dimensions. They have a higher heart rate (Kelly, 1980), resting heart rate, and higher systolic blood pressure (Lader, 1975), and elevated levels of fluctuation in electrodermal activity—a measure of physiological arousal (Lader, 1975; Lader & Wing, 1966). Moreover, as stated in chapter 3, HACDs experience an imbalance of certain neurotransmitters: an excess of MAO, epinephrine, norepinephrine, and dopamine, and a deficiency of serotonin. The evidence is not perfectly consistent on the last point (Zuckerman, 1991). These imbalances in neurotransmitters, which probably result from some combination of genetic predisposition and early childhood stress, produce a constant of high emotion: fear, anxiety, and arousal.

Behaviors can change the imbalance in neurotransmitters, thus having a very calming effect on a person. These can include healthy behaviors such as prayer and meditation or unhealthy behaviors such as frequent masturbation; long-term dependent relationships; and compulsive eating, exercising, and shopping. Many of these are learned at an early age. If parents teach children to eat when they are crying, cranky, bored, or irritated (or irritating), then they will likely use that same behavior throughout their lifetimes. If such people find a behavior on their own, such as exercising to relieve anxiety and emotion, that, too, will probably become compulsive due to the magnitude of relief that it provides.

As stated earlier, HACDs have a tendency to drink alcohol for its anxiety-reducing effects. If they take other drugs, they take prescription, sedative-type drugs (e.g., either tranquilizers or sleeping pills).

If they are not genetically predisposed to chemical dependency, they do not readily become dependent; however, if they abuse any mood-altering drug long enough, the addictive nature of the drug itself produces dependency.

Psychological Profile

Because HACDs are already in a state of excessive arousal, they do not seek additional stimulation through change, sensation seeking, risk-taking, or novelty of any kind. Novel situations are perceived as potentially threatening and are therefore avoided. Instead, HACDs seek highly predictable lifestyles emphasizing familiarity, long-term relationships, job stability, and nonrisk-taking activities.

Interpersonally, the majority of HACDs are careful, inhibited, and overly concerned about the thoughts and feelings of others and therefore tend toward "people-pleasing" behavior. They spend a great deal of time analyzing and thinking about what happens to them, usually concluding that anything negative is their fault. They tend to use perfectionism to reduce anxiety and to hide from their feelings.

Compared with SSCDs, HACDs are more inhibited in their social relationships, but they wish to be liked and often go to extremes to gain acceptance from others. They are less likely to escape from dysfunctional homes at an early age and to find social support from kindred spirits among their teen peer group. In their younger years, school phobia and hypochondriacal fears are not uncommon. Later, HACDs often excel at school and in other activities and find a sense of relief in achievement.

In more extreme situations, HACDs are likely to suffer from one or more of a variety of disorders, including generalized anxiety disorder, dysthymia, obsessive–compulsive disorders, and panic disorders with or without agoraphobia.

HACDs and Codependency

It is probably apparent to the reader that our description of the personalities of HACDs is extremely similar to our description of the anxiously attached, people-pleasing type of codependent described in chapter 4. In our first case example, Jim lost his mother at a young age and had an alcoholic father who was emotionally abusive. Either of these factors alone would be expected to have an extremely negative impact on a child's self-esteem, self-concept, ability to develop healthy affectional bonds with significant others, and ability to feel secure in the world. Together, these early experiences inevitably predispose an individual to a lifelong struggle against anxiety, insecurity, and a codependent lifestyle.

In Jim's case, he resorted to alcohol to relieve his pain and unfortunately—or perhaps fortunately—his genetic makeup and psychophysiology led inevitably to alcoholism as well as compulsive sexuality and compulsive workaholism. We say "fortunately" because without the relief of drugs and compulsive behaviors, Jim may have plunged into deep depression, perhaps resulting in suicide. Or, he might have been able to postpone treatment even longer had it not been for his drinking patterns.

Liz also suffered serious damage in her childhood bonding experience. She had two alcoholic parents who were not consistently available to her in any nurturing or supportive way. She was the "parentified" child, playing the role of mother not only to her siblings, but also to her own dysfunctional mother. Her father was guilty of perhaps the greatest betrayal of trust between a parent and child. His relationship with his daughter had sexual connotations and could be described as covert sexual abuse. The fact that the behavior was covert left Liz ambivalent and confused in her relationship with her father and with boys in her adolescence. On top of that, she suffered the sudden loss of her father, who, despite his betrayal, was loved deeply by her.

Liz developed into the classic caretaking codependent who found a modicum of purpose and meaning in life by giving up her own life to take care of others. She also found a sense of self-worth by excelling at her schoolwork and later on in her career. She also appears to have had an eating disorder. She found her greatest relief, however, in the oblivion of chemicals. Again, because she possessed a certain genetic predisposition, Liz was destined to become chemically dependent once she began to use alcohol to escape her shame and loneliness.

Conclusions

Excessive worry, lack of confidence, disturbed social relationships, excessive shame, depression, loneliness, and isolation—this is generally the reality of HACDs before they ever pick up a drink. Chemicals and, in many instances, other compulsive behaviors are initially used to relieve the pain. Although offering a temporary fix, the "cure" eventually becomes as great as the original problem. Soon, the addiction takes on a life of its own, compounding all of the unhappiness and misery and preventing an individual from ever instituting change. Thus, the first step in any recovery program must begin with the acceptance of one's chemical dependence and powerlessness. Only then can there be any hope or expectation of meaningful change. The next chapter deals with treatment and recovery for the HACD and the family.

References

Kelly, D. (1980). *Anxiety and emotions.* Springfield, IL: Charles C. Thomas.

Lader, M. H. (1975). The psychophysiology of anxious and depressed patient. In D. C. Fowles, (Ed.), *Clinical Applications of psychophysiology* (pp. 12–41). New York: Columbia University Press.

Lader, M. H., & Wing, L. (1966). *Physiological measures, sedative drugs and morbid anxiety.* London: Oxford University Press.

Zuckerman, M. (1991). *Psychobiology of personality.* New York: Cambridge University Press.

9

High Anxiety Chemical Dependents: Treatment and Recovery

In many ways, diagnosis of HACDs is more difficult than diagnosis of SSCDs because HACDs usually do not demonstrate the extreme behavior of SSCDs. Moreover, in early sobriety, almost all alcoholics display some of the symptoms of the HACD because of the nature of withdrawal. Thus, it is easy to confuse HACDs with uncomplicated CDs, that is, those who are biochemically balanced and who do not have extreme personality characteristics (see Fig. 3.2, chapter 3) and yet show high levels of anxiety due to withdrawal.

The HACD has a lesser degree of genetic predisposition to chemical dependency—they are influenced by both genetic and environmental factors. To summarize, the HACD is characterized by the following behaviors:

1. Low novelty seeking and risk-taking
2. High dependence on normal societal rewards
3. High harm avoidance, which discourages risk-taking and novelty seeking
4. A proclivity for single compulsive behaviors, most frequently eating disorders, excessive shopping and spending, overexercising, and workaholism.
5. Late chemical use and abuse (over the age of 25) and few chemical-related problems before the age of 30.
6. Lesser likelihood of a concomitant psychiatric disorder.

Although a definitive diagnosis of HACD may take 1 to 3 months or more into sobriety, a thorough history of the individual, combined with the PHQ and CBI, in most cases, gives a fairly good idea as to whether an individual is an HACD.

As just stated, HACDs showed low novelty-seeking behavior in the past. They generally "play it safe," tending to be rigid, orderly, and not likely to take significant risks.

They are apprehensive, pessimistic, and on edge much of the time. They are also prone to fatigue easily. They are socially sensitive, interpersonally available, eager to help others, and, in many instances, overly concerned about the thoughts and feelings of others.

Although HACDs are considerably more likely than the average person to have a compulsive behavior, they are less likely than the SSCD, and much less likely to engage in multiple compulsive behaviors. As noted earlier, if compulsive behaviors exist, they are likely to be ARCBs, such as excessive eating, spending, exercising, or workaholism. If there is a compulsion around sexuality, it is likely to be less risky and less dramatic than the behavior engaged in by the SSCD. Masturbation, pornography that can be viewed at home, and long-term romantic affairs are typical.

Interestingly, it is not uncommon for HACDs to show no evidence of compulsive behaviors at all during their active chemical dependency, only to have compulsions reappear in sobriety. In these instances, the compulsions are generally not immediately present, but become apparent between 6 months and 1 year into sobriety. Again, a thorough history that asks about sexual, food, school, and work habits and spending in childhood and adolescence can be invaluable.

Concerning psychiatric complications, the HACD is, by definition, anxious and mildly depressed (e.g., a sense of apprehension, dread, low self-esteem). In certain instances, the anxiety and depression are of a more serious nature, and a psychiatric evaluation to consider antidepressant medication is warranted. The more serious psychiatric diagnoses often seen among SSCDs (see chapter 7) are relatively uncommon among HACDs.

Short-term treatment goals for HACDs are the same as for SSCDs: to help them overcome their denial of their chemical dependency and to teach them coping mechanisms necessary to function adequately without resorting to chemical use.

Broadly speaking, long-term treatment goals include learning to live life without undue anxiety and depression, including learning to develop a degree of intimacy with others, an increased willingness to take more risks in life, and a greater enjoyment of life.

Case Study: Jim

A number of problems confront Jim's therapist. Jim must first come to terms with the fact that he is alcoholic and he must be helped to deal with the full implications of that acceptance. This is always difficult with an individual who has had a relatively *high bottom.*[1] This is particularly true when people have struggled with psychological symptoms before they abused alcohol or other drugs. Although therapists would like to have recovering individuals consciously accept their alcoholism and ask for a list of AA meetings, rarely does this occur.

Jim was not ready to accept the label alcoholic, but he was willing to abstain from alcohol during treatment. Jim also agreed to attend an early-recovery professional treatment group to help him make up his mind. It was important to have him attend a group in which there were other high bottom alcoholics with whom he could identify. To have him attend a group in which the majority of participants had progressed to a more serious level would most likely have been counterproductive. Jim would have felt too "different from those other people," and his resistance to acceptance of his alcoholism would have increased.

In addition, Jim was resistant to attending AA meetings. The therapist was patient with this reluctance and allowed Jim to develop a degree of trust before emphasizing the importance of AA. When the therapist was ready to emphasize AA, he helped Jim understand the difference between *abstinence* and *recovery* (or sobriety).[2] He briefly explained AA's philosophy of life, emphasized the importance of the friendships available in the program, and helped Jim connect with a person active in the program who would be an appropriate match (e.g., a same-sex person with a similar background and lifestyle and a member with a number of years of sobriety). Jim was told that he did not have to be convinced that he was an alcoholic to attend. The only requirement was his commitment to not drinking.

It was made clear to Jim that if he were to relapse, he would have to do whatever the therapist determined was necessary, or he would not be treated any longer. Depending on the circumstances, this requirement might include residential treatment in a recovery program, an intensive evening program (e.g., three to four evenings a week) or a combination of an early-recovery group and a definite commitment to AA, such as 90 meetings in 90 days.

Fortunately, Jim was able to abstain from alcohol. He began attending AA meetings and made progress during the first 3 months in recovery, especially in his increased social activities. It was helpful that Jim's chemical dependence

---

[1]For those less familiar with 12-step terminology, the word *bottom* refers to that time when a person finally asks for help but may not recognize that alcohol is a basic problem. Although not ready to admit that they are addicted, they usually attempt to comply with a request to stop using chemicals. A *high bottom* refers to such an occurrence before a serious medical, social, legal, family, financial, or job crisis occurs.

[2]*Abstinence* means not using chemicals. *Recovery* or *sobriety* means learning to live a happy and fulfilling life without chemicals. It provides the tools to meet life's challenges and difficulties without picking up a chemical.

had not progressed to the point that he had many practical problems to resolve (e.g., legal or family problems). He was also motivated and came into therapy of his own accord (with coaxing from his wife) and was looking for help with specific psychological and interpersonal problems. The therapist also took every opportunity to suggest to Jim that his problems and unhappiness resulted, in part, at least, from his chemical use.

Jim did not find it too difficult to stop drinking and made sure that he stayed busy on weekends so he would not "be tempted." His wife, Kathy, reported that his mood was improved and that he was more patient.

One problem that the therapist had to address quickly was the ongoing relationship Jim maintained with a woman at work. Unfortunately, circumstances made this a very complicated issue with no easy answers because it was the kind of issue that could threaten Jim's recovery, his marriage, and his livelihood.

The first step was to determine the nature of Jim's relationship at work. Given his history of extramarital affairs, it is very likely that Jim is a sex and romance addict. The therapist explored this possibility by considering the nature of Jim's affairs; the role of sex, especially at the beginning of the affairs; the extent to which Jim used poor judgment while involved in the affairs; and Jim's feelings about his commitment to his wife. It was clear that Jim's affairs were primarily sexual, that he consistently used poor judgment and was indiscreet, and that he was seriously committed to his wife.

The therapist's goal was to help Jim understand that he must live his life honestly to find serenity and happiness. This meant that he must ultimately end all extramarital affairs or leave the marriage. Jim had no doubt that he wanted to stay in his marriage.

Once that decision was made, the therapist helped Jim decide how and when he intended to end the relationship at work. The therapist also began to educate Jim about sex and romance addiction and helped him to realize that his behavior was not caused by his unhappiness in his marriage or by moral weakness. The therapist discussed the availability of SLAA and other related 12-step programs. Again, as with chemical use, the therapist left the decision to Jim but insisted that the possibility of a more rigorous program would be needed if Jim was not able to change his behavior.

Jim was very concerned that ending the relationship at work in a precipitous fashion could result in his lovers calling his wife, could cause him to lose his job, or could end in a legal action against him, such as for sexual harassment. Interestingly, sex addicts like Jim usually get involved with people who are not serious threats to their marriages. Many times the affairs are with other sex addicts or persons who have had other affairs. Thus, the relationship is not a serious "love affair" for the other person either and ending the relationship does not result in the feared negative consequences. However, even though patients generally exaggerate their fears, the possibility of negative consequences exists, and, thus, the therapist must respect this position and make sure patients make their own decisions as to exactly how their relationships will be terminated.

The therapist prepared Jim for any difficulties he might face as a result of his ending the relationship. The most likely negative outcome would be that the other person would try to maintain the relationship. The therapist supported Jim in his commitment to change and reminded him that his number one priority was honesty even if it meant leaving his job if he could not end the affair while still working there. It was also pointed out to Jim that there was also the possibility that once his wife was informed of his sex and love addiction at a later point in therapy, she might insist that he have no further contact with his lover, so that, again, he might have to leave his job.

In Jim's case, the problem was fortunately resolved with relatively few complications. The woman at work was married and had no intentions of leaving her marriage. Although she was disappointed that Jim was ending the affair, she accepted his decision. Moreover, the two of them did not come into close contact on the job on a regular basis. Even though the therapist had warned Jim of the likelihood of withdrawal from his sexual relationship, Jim was surprised by the degree of loneliness, longing, and vulnerability he experienced. The therapist assured him that he did not miss the person as much as he missed the security he got from being in an addictive relationship.

Regarding Jim's diagnosis, it was clear that he was not an SSCD. Moreover, it was almost certain that he was not an uncomplicated alcoholic whose psychological and emotional problems were merely a by-product of his chemical addiction. His family history suggests otherwise. His father's alcoholism and emotional abuse, the death of his mother at an early age, the ensuing emotional problems that were never addressed, and his history of codependent relationships with women all strongly suggest HACD.

After Jim had been in therapy for some months, Kathy decided that she, too, wanted to be in therapy to deal with some of her own problems, especially those related to having grown up in an alcoholic family herself. She also began to attend Alanon. Fortunately, Kathy saw a therapist who was able to work closely with Jim's therapist, and thus the therapists were able to jointly determine when it would be appropriate to begin couples therapy. Four months into Jim's sobriety, it was decided that Jim and Kathy would attend individual therapy every other week and that on alternate weeks they both would meet with Jim's therapist.

In the treatment of Jim and Kathy, the therapy had to address Jim's affairs. Fortunately, in this case, Jim was able to do so fairly early in the therapy. Kathy's initial reaction was quite naturally anger, hurt, and a sense of betrayal that lasted for a few days. With the help of her individual therapist, however, she was able to see, in retrospect, that there had been many signs of Jim's infidelity but that she had not allowed herself to see them because she did not want to deal with them. Thus, much of her anger was actually directed at herself, not because she felt she was in any way to blame for Jim's behavior (she was not) but because she had not dealt with it sooner.

After Jim got over the worst of his withdrawal from his sexual addiction,[3] and after working through the initial drama of sharing his sexual history with Kathy, he felt good. He reported that he worried less and felt more optimistic about life. Jim and Kathy reported that they were also getting along better, and there was no real conflict. They were not spending a lot of time together, however, and there was, as yet, no significant increase in their level of emotional intimacy.

After about 6 months, Jim suddenly began to feel more anxious and depressed. This is not unusual, for HACDs begin to reexperience many of their symptoms after the "pink cloud" of early recovery begins to diminish. This can occur at any time during the first 2 years of sobriety, although it is more likely to occur sometime after 3 months and before 1 year. In Jim's case, symptoms reemerged relatively early in sobriety, perhaps triggered, in part, by the anniversary of his mother's death.

Because Jim was regularly attending AA meetings, was developing a support system in the fellowship, and was not struggling with drinking, the therapist felt it was appropriate to deal with the damage done to Jim in childhood and to help him understand how it contributed to his insecurity, excessive worry, and codependence. Jim responded well to this stage of therapy and made rapid progress.

Concerning his marriage, it was clearly observed that Jim and Kathy had drifted apart and remained apart for many years; they were two people living in the same space but very rarely touching each other. They truly cared about each other, but there were little intimacy, little romance, and a lot of avoidance and dishonesty.

Kathy always tried to be thoughtful and understanding, often at her own expense. Thus, she made few demands on Jim and lost her own sense of will and autonomy within her relationship, despite being a strong, outspoken, and competent woman in other areas of her life. Jim had become bored with the ever-caring "good wife" who never challenged him and who had lost her own identity. In the marriage, Jim became more self-centered, a trait that did not especially please him.

Kathy had become quietly resentful and had shut down in many ways, particularly sexually. It was not a matter of "holding back"; it was simply a matter of feeling unappreciated as a person and stifling much of her emotional life as well as her sexual life.

For most couples whose marriage is troubled, lack of sex is almost always an issue and can provide the therapist with very important information at the beginning of therapy. Some couples remain very sexually active, even though there are serious problems in the marriage, however, these are the exception. Jim and Kathy's teenage sons, Matthew (17) and John (15), came in for an early session with the parents. They both appeared to be functioning well at the time. Both were good students, had active social lives, and were happy about their father's sobriety. There was no evidence that they themselves were using

---

[3]It is difficult to predict how long withdrawal from a compulsive sexual disorder will last. The worst of it is generally over within 1 to 3 months, although, for certain individuals, some aspects of it can linger for a year or more.

chemicals. Both had some awareness of the nature of chemical dependence and were aware that they were at high risk themselves because of the family history of alcoholism.

Although it is highly probable that each of these boys would find it helpful someday to be in therapy to deal with whatever damage was done to them as a result of the family dysfunction, there was no evidence at this time of the presence of any symptoms. Therefore, it was decided that there was no reason for them to be in regular therapy but that they should attend a family session intermittently to see how things were going for them. In addition, Jim and Kathy were told to watch their boys for signs of chemical abuse, social withdrawal, sleep disturbance, mood swings, or any other signs of possible depression.

Within 6 months, Jim and Kathy were able to terminate therapy. Jim continued attending AA regularly and Kathy continued with Alanon. They felt that their marriage wounds were not entirely healed, but they felt that, for the first time, they understood the value of honesty and intimacy in their lives and recognized what it took to make their marriage work. They had learned to set time aside just to be together and to talk, and they had learned to have fun together, to be romantic, and to begin to realize that they had to work to understand each other.

Their sons continued to do well and had no apparent symptoms or desire to be in therapy. Given the years of dysfunction in the marriage, it would be hard to imagine that the sons were not affected. No therapeutic work can be done, however, unless people are feeling emotional pain or the significant persons in their lives are disturbed by their behavior. It is likely that as these boys get older and get married themselves, the unfinished business from the early family dysfunction will show itself in their own marriage; however, until there are problems, there is no rationale for therapy.

Case History: Liz

Although, in certain instances, it can be difficult to differentiate between the SSCD and the HACD, in the case of Liz, no such difficulty existed. She was obviously an HACD.

Given Liz's family of origin history and the degree of social isolation that preceded her chemical abuse, the therapist was attuned to the strong probability of psychological and emotional dysfunction. The most likely issues were low self-esteem, poor social skills, anxiety, a codependent lifestyle, and possible depression. The extenuating circumstances (e.g., taking care of her mother, being responsible for her brothers) were likely contributing factors, as was an unconscious collaboration in the family dynamics that suited Liz's personality and emotional dysfunction. This collaboration allowed her to withdraw from life in a way that both made sense and gave her esteem within the family.

Liz's history suggested she would have much to do if she hoped to live a genuinely healthy and productive life in the future. Compared with many others, however, her early recovery program was relatively uncomplicated. She did not associate with people who abused chemicals. She did not often find herself in social situations in which alcohol use was the norm, and she did not go to nightclubs or bars (in 12-step language, "people, places, and things"). Moreover, she did not have to deal with a dysfunctional marriage or family life. She was a competent worker, had a secure job, and so did not have to worry about earning a living.

The one complication was her relationship at work. Although it was obvious that the relationship was unhealthy in the long run, the question of the timing in dealing with it had to be considered. Because it was one of the few relationships in Liz's life that were important to her and because it was sporadic and did not involve drinking activities, it was not felt to be an immediate threat to her sobriety.

Therefore, it was decided to postpone dealing with this issue until later. Early recovery focused on attending AA meetings, getting a 12-step sponsor, joining an all-female early-recovery therapy group, and individual supportive therapy with a woman therapist.

Concerning her long-term recovery, Liz had many serious and difficult issues to deal with. She had led a socially isolated existence, failing to establish any healthy friendships with other women or men. She missed many of the normal socialization experiences of childhood and adolescence and, as a result, lacked appropriate social skills. Her shame-based self-concept resulted in low self-esteem. Her father's inappropriate, covert sexual interest in her was quite confusing, and her sporadic sex life with her lover brought on feelings of intense shame.

As a parentified child, Liz never had the opportunity to develop firm boundaries, a clear self-concept, or an ability to know and understand her own feelings or experiences. She was also deprived of the joy and security that result from a childhood of healthy bonding experiences with adults who could be trusted to take care of her.

As discussed in chapter 4, these situations result in a codependent pattern in which the people find it difficult to feel secure in life and to be aware of their own needs and feelings. Thus, Liz found it easier to be concerned with other people's struggles rather than with her own. The therapist was able to help Liz recognize this about herself and to help her shift her attention to her own needs. She also helped Liz understand and deal with the anxiety and shame that she experienced as she began to focus on her own needs. Her therapist helped her understand that her anxiety and shame resulted from her attempt to challenge the family "rule" that she and her needs were unimportant and that her purpose in life was to meet the emotional needs of her parents and brothers.

As is typical in many such cases, this awareness resulted in Liz's experiencing anger and hostility, of which she was hardly aware. Much of this hostility was directed at her therapist. This was done indirectly at first, resulting in lateness and missed appointments. Gradually, Liz's expressions of anger at the therapist became more direct, and she began to express mistrust of her therapist, criticizing her for "not caring enough." Liz's therapist continued to be firm but not defensive and was particularly vigilant, realizing that Liz was extremely vulnerable and at risk of a relapse. Rather than interpreting Liz's behavior, which would have resulted in Liz's feeling discounted, the therapist allowed Liz to be angry at her and encouraged her to attend more 12-step meetings and stay in close touch with her sponsor and support system. Gradually, Liz's anger at her therapist subsided, and she began to understand the real source of her anger.

As part of recovery, Liz eventually had to look at the relationship with her lover. Fortunately, as she began to look at her emotional needs, the unhealthy aspects of the relationship became obvious to her. She knew that eventually she wanted a relationship that offered her more in the way of emotional intimacy and commitment.

In addition, the fact that her lover was married made the relationship inherently dishonest and thereby a threat to her recovery program. Unfortunately, the intellectual aspect of this insight did not make it easy for Liz to make the final break. The therapist had to encourage, rehearse, and support her through this ordeal as Liz was able to handle it. Pushing too hard or fast could have threatened the therapeutic alliance, and Liz may have dropped out of therapy or lied to her therapist about the liaison.

In the process of ending and grieving the loss of the relationship, Liz began to grieve many other losses. These included the lack of a normal family life or a normal social life, her codependence, and her own chemical addiction. Although this process of grieving losses often does not occur until a number of years into recovery, in some cases, as with Liz, it can begin much sooner, especially if the losses are great and if some specific loss occurs early in recovery that can serve as a catalyst.

Although the grieving process can vary greatly in length and intensity, for Liz it was an extremely intense period that lasted approximately 2 months. During that time, Liz became depressed, although she was able to go to work and function. Periods of sleeplessness, hopelessness, and anxiety were common. She was able to cope by attending more 12-step meetings and talking about her experiences, by seeing her therapist twice weekly, and by making regular phone contacts with 12-step program people. Had her depression became so intense that she was unable to be with people, antidepressant medication would probably have been considered.

As a result of this grieving period, Liz could begin to accept her past and to begin to develop realistic hopes for her future. She was able to begin to let go of her repressed resentment and hostility, and, instead, experienced appropriate feelings of sadness and loss. She made a realistic appraisal of her surviving family members (her brothers) and realized that she would someday want to attempt to reestablish contact with them. However, she felt that such an attempt would be too risky at this early stage of her recovery.

As a final step in Liz's therapy, the therapist explored the likelihood of the emergence or reemergence of compulsive disorders in Liz's life. Although the possibility of love addiction was considered, Liz's relationship with her lover had never been motivated by romance or sexuality. Although the HACD does not seek a sexual-romantic high in the same way as the SSCD, there is, nevertheless, a certain degree of intrigue, romance, and sexual excitement that motivates the relationship. In Liz's case, these factors were not operative. Instead, she responded to what she perceived to be the kindness, gentleness, and caring of her friend. Sex did not motivate her except that her friend wanted the relationship to be sexual, and it did help her to feel closer to him. She would have been just as satisfied with the relationship, however, if there had been no sexual contact. In this instance, the relationship was a classic case of one of the many forms of codependence.

The two types of behaviors that were a potential threat to Liz's recovery included eating and work. Liz had a history of being overweight. She would go on crash diets, and her weight would go up and down. At this time, eating presented no problems; however, Liz's therapist discussed this issue with her and discussed the danger signals to be aware of.

Regarding her work habits, Liz continued to allow her work to be the primary source of her feelings of competence and self-esteem. Given the heretofore emptiness in her life, this was not surprising. Liz's entire program was designed to help her develop healthy social relationships in her life, and until that had time to develop further, it was not wise to insist on any radical changes in Liz's work habits, assuming they did not keep her from her program commitments.

With these matters addressed, Liz was discharged from individual treatment for a 2-month period. After that time, she would be seen again to determine how well she was doing, what kinds of problems may have arisen, and whether she was continuing to follow her recovery program.

After the 2-month break in individual and group therapy, Liz was seen again. She looked well and reported that she was continuing to do well in her program. She was quite active in AA and had developed a network of friendships. She admitted that she did miss her old boyfriend, but recognized that the relationship had been unhealthy.

Another session was scheduled with Liz for 2 months later, but, after about a month, she called the therapist to request an emergency session. She reported that she was anxious and frightened, struggling with a sense of dread. She could not sleep, was unable to make decisions, and could not concentrate. She had been socially withdrawn and even found it difficult to attend meetings. Although she had not felt any strong temptation to drink, she was not feeling particularly confident about her sobriety.

When questioned about the possible reasons for her depression, Liz was uncertain. She did report feeling badly, however, because she had written to both of her brothers, bringing them up to date on her life and saying that she would like to reconnect with them. She had not, however, received a response, even though it had been more than 3 weeks.

The therapist felt that prior to further exploration of Liz's reactions to her brothers, she needed to address the depression. Because Liz was not suicidal and because she was willing to contact her sponsor and other program people to make sure she got to meetings, it was decided that hospitalization was not necessary. Antidepressant medication seemed appropriate, however, given the extent of Liz's symptomatology. Liz had already been educated about the biochemical aspects of depression and the difference between antidepressants and the dangerously addictive, mood-altering minor tranquilizers (benzodiazepenes). She agreed to a psychiatric consultation, which supported the diagnosis of major depression. Liz began to take an antidepressant, and her symptoms alleviated significantly after a month (she took this medication for approximately 1 year). After a month on antidepressants, she dealt in therapy with the issue with her brothers. Again, Liz was discharged and returned in 2 months. Liz was doing very well at that time, and her therapy was terminated.

Currently, Liz has been sober for almost 5 years. She has continued in the same job and is dating a man rather seriously. She struggles with depressive symptoms on occasion, but has never had to be on antidepressants again.

Summary

In this chapter we examined the ideas and principles used in the treatment and recovery of HACDs. The respective recoveries of two HACDs were explored in detail. Although these individuals differed in many important details in their lives (e.g., one was a married man with two children and a normal social life, whereas the second was a single woman who lived an isolated and reclusive existence), they each shared the common characteristics typical of the HACD. Each suffered from anxiety and low self-esteem. Each had many of the character traits of a typical codependent. Each came from an unhealthy family of origin. Both were involved in unhealthy relationships at work, a characteristic not uncommon among HACDs because they are needy individuals who find it difficult to maintain appropriate boundaries in relationships.

Proper diagnosis of the HACD is fairly straightforward and involves a good clinical history, combined with the PHQ and the CBI. When making the appropriate diagnosis of the HACD, the more difficult issue is discriminating between the HACD and the uncomplicated alcoholic. This results from the fact that in early sobriety, uncomplicated alcoholics show many of the some characteristics of the high-anxiety type.

Although HACDs have a number of problems that must be addressed in therapy, the number one priority must be the chemical dependency. Psychological change and growth are impossible as long as active chemical dependency continues. Perhaps the greatest mistake that a therapist can make is to believe that other issues in the HACD's life are more important than the chemical dependency or that chemicals are merely a symptom of other problems and that if these other problems are dealt with, the person will easily stop the chemicals. Although psychological problems may have initially contributed to abusive chemical use, once addiction occurs, it has a life of its own.

Of course, in dealing with HACDs, a therapist must often be patient and accept patients' reluctance to fully accept the dependency. The commitment to abstinence, however, must occur early in therapy, along with a clear agreement as to what steps must be taken if patients cannot maintain abstinence on their own.

As is typical of the majority of HACDs, both Jim and Liz suffered symptoms of clinical depression. Although antidepressant medication is sometimes an important and necessary ingredient in treating the HACD (as was the case for Liz), therapists and physicians must always be judicious in recommending antidepressants to a recovering person (mood-altering medication, particularly the benzodiazepines, are very seldom appropriate for a chemically dependent person).

In the cases presented in this chapter, both individuals struggled with compulsive behaviors. Jim was a sex and romance addict. Naturally, this complicated his recovery and made it more difficult. It threatened his marriage and his job, although, in Jim's case, these problems were resolved without losing his marriage or his employment. He suffered, however, the painful withdrawal (feelings of loneliness, vulnerability, etc.) that is quite typical of the recovering sex and romance addict.

Liz was not a sex and romance addict, but was codependent and vulnerable to anyone showing her kindness and attention. Thus, she experienced less difficulty withdrawing from her relationship than did Jim. Liz was probably compulsive in her work, and her history suggested that she was at some risk of developing a compulsion about food. Liz was told some of the warning signs of an eating disorder, and as she became less isolated in her recovery, she began to find sources of self-esteem other than competence at work. Although there are no guarantees that Liz will not experience more difficult struggles with these or other compulsive disorders at some point, she is, at least, aware of her vulnerability and will hopefully seek appropriate help if needed. In both cases, it was obvious that family of origin issues are important in long-term recovery. Chemical dependency is strongly related to the family of origin because of both genetic and psychological factors. Individuals coming from families with chemical dependency appear to seek each other out and tend to reinforce each other's unhealthy patterns of behavior. Thus, it is important to include current family members and, when possible, family of origin members in the recovery of the CD. Without such inclusion, the possibility of long-term recovery and a healthy, productive life is extremely limited.

Liz's relationship with her brothers was quite intense, even though she was not in constant contact with them. Their lack of response to her (which she interpreted as rejection) sent her into an emotional tailspin and required an intense medication intervention to stabilize her.

Finally, in both cases, the importance of the family of origin and current family was stressed. Chemical dependency does not occur in a vacuum, and individuals do not recover in a vacuum. Although family members are not the cause of chemical dependency and compulsive behaviors, they are involved in two ways. First, certain individuals are attracted to CDs. In this case, someone, most likely from an addicted family of origin, is unconsciously seeking an addicted relationship. Second, a person may be psychologically unable to deal with an intimate relationship and unconsciously seeks a relationship that can never be intimate. Either way, the family members are an important source of corroborating information, and, even more important, they are a vital ingredient in the recovery of the CD and the family system.

10

Summary and Conclusions

In this book we attempt to integrate research findings in the area of the biochemistry of the brain, typology of CDs, and clinical experience with chemical dependency and codependency. More important, we provide a framework that allows the clinician to more adequately assess a patient, set diagnostic and treatment priorities, and develop a treatment plan. We present an overview of treatment issues and specific guidelines for the therapist to be aware of and to use to assist the patient as he or she struggles with recovery.

The research presented here is limited. Despite the shortcomings in the data presented, four conclusions appear warranted:

1. The number of CDs with compulsive behaviors dominate clinical practice.
2. At least one third of the CDs with compulsive behaviors experience multiple compulsive behaviors.
3. The most common compulsive behaviors are sex and romance, working, and shopping and spending.
4. Men are more likely to be SSCDs, and women are more likely to be HACDs.

Despite the billions of dollars spent by both the federal and state governments in an effort to fight the "drug war," it is our belief that the number of CDs and the number of CDs with compulsive behaviors have increased significantly in the last 20 years. An explanation of the increase in SSCDs and the even greater increase in HACDs requires some speculation and is discussed. It is our contention that:

1. The number of uncomplicated alcoholics has decreased.
2. The number of SSCDs with a dominant genetic predisposition has probably increased slightly.
3. The number of HACDs with both a genetic and a greater environmental influence has increased significantly.

These changes, without specific numbers, are represented in Fig. 10.1

In closing, it is important to speculate about the impact of recent biochemical and genetic findings on national drug and alcohol policy. To date, it is disturbing to note that, that despite the "war on drugs," aimed most significantly at drug interdiction, the availability of illicit drugs has not noticeably decreased and the number of chemically dependent individuals has not changed appreciably (if anything, it has probably increased). One would think that after years of trying a failed strategy (in this case, drug interdiction), new and different strategies would be tried. But the question is, if chemical dependency and compulsive behaviors have a biochemical and genetic basis what new startegies should be tried?

Any theory or strategy is based on the assumptions that are made in the beginning. If it is assumed that the availability of alcohol and other drugs will remain in our society and that many, if not most, people are going to at least try these chemicals, then there will always be addiction and related compulsive behaviors. Some individuals, particularly SSCDs, are exceptionally vulnerable, and addiction occurs with little chemical stimulation. As the society in which we live becomes more strained, especially with the continued breakdown of the family, the number of HACDs will continue to increase.

Because of these assumptions, any prevention theory based on teaching people not to use chemicals or to use them in moderation will be of very limited success. For the individual with a genetic predisposition for chemical dependency, even moderate amounts of chemicals stimulate the addiction. The only answer for a person with a genetic predisposition is total abstinence.

This is not to say, however, that education and other prevention strategies are not useful. Chemical dependency education can be an effective tool in

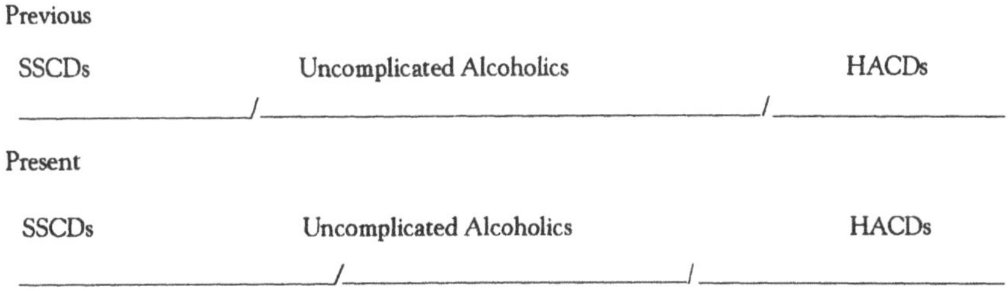

FIG. 10.1. The proportional relationship of SSCDs, uncomplcated alcoholics, and HACDs.

intervention, the second level of treatment. The ever-present denial of the addict (and family members) is based on the stigma surrounding addiction. A person without stigma finds it much easier to see the truth. Persons (or families) well educated on chemical dependency as a disease will recognize it (or have it pointed out to them) in its early stages and will not have to go through years of misery and failure. Twelve-step programs are filled with young people who have been the benefactors of professional intervention strategies. This is intervention at its best.

The majority of individuals with a predisposition will, however, experience chemical dependency and compulsive behaviors. In this book, a road map for the interested professional is provided, but this road map is a primer, a starting point for those who want to be most effective in treating chemically dependent individuals with compulsive behaviors. We hope that the subject of this book will generate additional research and clinical curiosity. If it accomplishes this goal, then we have realized our own dream.

APPENDIX A

PERSONAL HISTORY QUESTIONNAIRE

DATE COMPLETED____ AGE____ SEX____ RACE ____

Please try to answer all of the following question as best you can. Any question that does not apply, please indicate by writing NA.

Section A. This section deals with chemical use (alcohol and other drugs). If you are in recovery from chemical dependence, answer as you would have during your active chemical use.

	Never	*Seldom*	*Some-times*	*Often*	*Always*
1. I use chemicals more than I intend.	____	____	____	____	____
2. I have attempted to control or reduce my chemical use, but have been unable to do so.	____	____	____	____	____
3. I spend a great deal of time in chemical-related activities.	____	____	____	____	____
4. I have been unable to fulfill obligations because of my chemical use.	____	____	____	____	____
5. I have given up certain social, occupational, or recreational activities because of chemical use.	____	____	____	____	____
6. I have experienced social, emotional, legal, or physical problems because of chemical use.	____	____	____	____	____
7. Over time, it takes more of the chemical(s) to achieve the desired results.	____	____	____	____	____
8. I suffer irritability, nervousness, or other signs when I cannot take chemicals.	____	____	____	____	____

	Never	*Seldom*	*Some-times*	*Often*	*Always*
9. I take chemicals to relieve uncomfortable feelings.	____	____	____	____	____

Section B. If you answered 3 or more questions in the last two columns (*Often* or *Always*) in Section A , please complete the next 12 questions. If not, proceed to Section C.

1. The age I started having social, health legal, financial, or occupational problems with alcohol or other drugs. ____
2. The age of my first alcohol/drug treatment contact or the age I first attended AA or NA meeting. ____
3. Total number of alcohol/drug treatment experiences prior to completion of this questionnaire. ____
4. I get into fights or arguments with family or friends when drinking/using.

   infrequently____ sometimes____ frequently____
5. I have alcohol/drug-related arrests on my record. Yes____ No____
6. I went on benders (got drunk/high at least 2 days in a row):

   infrequently____ sometimes____ frequently____
7. I have been diagnosed as having cirrhosis/liver disease or other alcohol/drug related diseases. Yes____ No____
8. At times, I went for days or even weeks without using alcohol/drugs.

   infrequently____ sometimes____ frequently____
9. I feel guilty about alcohol/drug use or related behaviors.

   infrequently____ sometimes____ frequently____
10. Age at which you started regular use of the following:

    ____ cigarettes

    ____ alcohol

    ____ other drugs
11. Past use of alcohol and other drugs; check all that you have used:

Legal:	Illegal:
____ alcohol	____ sedatives
____ nicotine	____ opiates
Prescriptions:	____ amphetamines
____ sedatives	____ hallucinogens
____ amphetamines	____ marijuana
____ opiates	____ cocaine/crack
____ other	____ other

12. If in recovery, how long? Years____

Section C. Please answer each of the following questions as best as you can.

13. Check all that apply to your mother.
    ____ alcoholic/drug addicted
    ____ arrested
    ____ engaged in behavior that could have resulted in arrest
    ____ experienced periods of depression
14. Check all that apply to your father.
    ____ alcoholic/drug addicted
    ____ arrested
    ____ engaged in behavior that could have resulted in arrest
    ____ experienced periods of depression
15. The group I most closely identified with when I was in high school:
    ____ athletes ____ academics
    ____ wild bunch ____ other, specify ____________
16. As a child, I think I was sexually abused. ____ Yes ____No
17. As a child, I think I was physically abused. ____Yes ____No

PERSONAL HISTORY QUESTIONNAIRE

Scoring Instructions

Section A. To score Section A, which determines the degree of chemical dependency, complete the following computation:

1. Assign a number to each of the frequency categories at the top of the page, as follows: assign 1 to *Never;* 2 to *Seldom;* 3 to *Sometimes;* 4 to *Often;* and 5 to *Always.*
2. Next, go down the page and assign those numbers to the responses to each of the nine questions.
3. Total the scores for Section A.
4. A total score for Section A of more than 12 indicates a high probability of chemical dependency.

Section B. Score Section B and C, which determines if the respondent is a sensation seeker chemical dependent (SSCD) or a high-anxiety chemical dependent (HACD).

1. Score: 2 for less then 27 years old and -2 for 27 or older.

2. Score: 2 for less then 27 years old and -2 for 27 or older.
3. Score: 1 for each prior treatment. If respondent is under 27 years old, multiply score by 2.
4. Score: Infrequently -2; Sometimes 0; Frequently 2.
5. Score: Yes 2; No -2.
6. Score: Infrequently 2; Sometimes 0; Frequently -2
7. Score: Yes -2; No 2
8. Score: Infrequently -2; Sometimes 0; Frequently 2.
9. Score: Infrequently 2; Sometimes 0; Frequently -2.
10. Score: 2 for less then 21 years old and -2 for 21 or older.
11. Score: 2 for any illegal drug use, - 2 for only legal alcohol and other drug use.
12. No score

Section C.

13. Score: -2 for each Yes answer; 2 for each No answer.
14. Score: 2 for each Yes answer; -2 for each No answer.
15. Score: 2 for athletes or wild bunch; -2 for academic or other.
16. Score: 2 for Yes; -2 for No.
17. Score: 2 for Yes; -2 for No.

After the scores have been computed, add the score for the respondent. A plus score identifies a sensation seeker chemical dependent (SSCD), and a negative score identifies a high-anxiety chemical dependent (HACD). The higher the number (either positive or negative) identifies the location on the continuum below.

Score:

HACD	NEITHER	SSCD
-15	0	+15

APPENDIX B

COMPULSIVE BEHAVIOR INVENTORY

Please answer the following questions to the best of your ability. There are no right or wrong answers and no judgments on you about the answers you provide. This inventory will be strictly confidential and will not be shared with anyone without your permission.

	Never	*Seldom*	*Some-times*	*Often*	*Always*
A. Shopping and Spending:					
1. I shop when I feel happy or sad.	____	____	____	____	____
2. I spend more then I can afford on shopping sprees.	____	____	____	____	____
3. My credit cards are usually charged to the limit.	____	____	____	____	____
4. My spending sprees cause me or my family problems.	____	____	____	____	____
5. I think about shopping or buying things.	____	____	____	____	____

6. Although I do not struggle with shopping and spending thoughts or behaviors at the present, I have in the past. ____Yes ____No

B. Exercise:					
1. I exercise when I am bored, happy, feel bad, and even when I am sick.	____	____	____	____	____
2. When I attempt to resist exercising, there is a sense of mounting tension that can be relieved by exercising.	____	____	____	____	____
3. I feel uncomfortable if I miss my exercise routine.	____	____	____	____	____

	Never	*Seldom*	*Some-times*	*Often*	*Always*
4. Family or friends believe that my exercise time is consuming or interferes with my life or normal routine.	____	____	____	____	____
5. Even when I am not exercising, I think about it.	____	____	____	____	____

6. Although I do not struggle with exercise thoughts or behaviors at the present, I have in the past. ____Yes ____No

C. Work:

	Never	*Seldom*	*Some-times*	*Often*	*Always*
1. I work over 50 hours a week.	____	____	____	____	____
2. My family or friends think I work too much.	____	____	____	____	____
3. I have health or medical problems related to my work (stress, high blood pressure, low sex drive, etc.).	____	____	____	____	____
4. Work has interfered with my sexual, family, or social life.	____	____	____	____	____
5. Work helps me escape from an unpleasant situation at home.	____	____	____	____	____

6. Although I do not struggle with work thoughts or behaviors at the present, I have in the past. ____Yes ____No

D. Eating Habits

	Never	*Seldom*	*Some-times*	*Often*	*Always*
1. I go on rigid diets or go for periods in which I don't eat, even though I am not overweight.	____	____	____	____	____
2. I eat large amounts and then regret it, because I have a constant fear of gaining weight or becoming fat.	____	____	____	____	____

	Never	*Seldom*	*Some-times*	*Often*	*Always*
3. I eat in secret so that others will not know how much I eat.	____	____	____	____	____
4. My eating habits distress me and I feel fat or overweight.	____	____	____	____	____
5. I have made myself vomit or I have used laxatives or diet pills to lose weight.	____	____	____	____	____

6. Although I do not struggle with eating thoughts or behaviors at the present, I have in the past. ____Yes ____No

E. Gambling:

	Never	*Seldom*	*Some-times*	*Often*	*Always*
1. I bet more then I can afford.	____	____	____	____	____
2. My family or friends think that I gamble too much.	____	____	____	____	____
3. I speculate on the stock market or on investments.	____	____	____	____	____
4. I hide how much I gamble from others.	____	____	____	____	____
5. I think about gambling even when I am not gambling or my thoughts about gambling make me uncomfortable.	____	____	____	____	____

6. Although I do not struggle with gambling thoughts or behaviors at the present, I have in the past. ____Yes ____No

F. Taking Things

	Never	*Seldom*	*Some-times*	*Often*	*Always*
1. I take things from work, stores, or other places, even if I don't need them and I have money to pay for them.	____	____	____	____	____
2. I experience tension or excitement before taking something.	____	____	____	____	____

	Never	Seldom	Some-times	Often	Always
3. I feel a sense of satisfaction or relief when I take something.	____	____	____	____	____
4. When I take something, it is generally not preplanned.	____	____	____	____	____
5. Even when I am not taking something, I think about it.	____	____	____	____	____

6. Although I do not struggle with taking things thoughts or behaviors at the present, I have in the past. ____Yes ____No

G. Sex, Love, and Romantic Relationships:

	Never	Seldom	Some-times	Often	Always
1. I have had affairs outside of my primary relationship (marriage, or live-in relationship).	____	____	____	____	____
2. I have the urge to sexually expose myself, cross-dress, observe someone sexually, or do sexual behaviors that could get me into trouble.	____	____	____	____	____
3. I worry that someone will find out about my sexual behavior or romantic relationship.	____	____	____	____	____
4. I fall in love easily and think sexual thoughts more than most people.	____	____	____	____	____
5. I buy or read sexually explicit books, masturbate frequently, visit porn shops, or visit strip shows.	____	____	____	____	____

6. Although I do not struggle with sex, love, and relationship thoughts or behaviors at the present, I have in the past. ____Yes ____No

COMPLUSIVE BEHAVIOR INVENTORY

Scoring Instructions

It is not unusual for a chemical dependent to have one or more compulsive behaviors. In addition, the person may have both consecutive and concurrent compulsive behaviors. Question 6 in each behavior category provides insight into the possibility of a past compulsive behavior.

Although the inventory should not be considered conclusive, it assists the therapist in identifying behavior areas for further discussion. To score the Compulsive Behavior Inventory, complete the following computation:

1. Assign a number to each of the frequency categories at the top of the page, as follows: assign 1 to *Never;* 2 to *Seldom;* 3 to *Sometimes;* 4 to *Often;* and 5 to *Always.*
2. Next, go down the page and assign those numbers to the responses in each of the behavior categories (e.g., Shopping and Spending, Exercising, etc.).
3. Total the scores in each of the behavior categories.
4. A total score in any behavior category over 14, or any 4 (*Often*) or 5 (*Always*) response, indicates a high likelihood of a compulsive behavior.

Author Index

Subject Index